It's All About
JESUS

EDWIN WILE

Guardian
B O O K S

Belleville, Ontario, Canada

It's All About Jesus

Copyright © 2021, Edwin Wile

All Scripture quotations, unless otherwise specified, are from *The Holy Bible, King James Version.* Copyright © 1977, 1984, Thomas Nelson Inc., Publishers.

Scriptures marked NKJV are taken from the New King James Version. Copyright © 1979, 1980, 1982. Thomas Nelson Inc., Publishers.

Cataloguing data available from Library and Archives Canada

ISBN: 978-1-4600-1315-1
LSI Edition: 978-1-4600-1316-8
E-book ISBN: 978-1-4600-1317-5
(E-book available from the Kindle Store, KOBO and the iBooks Store)

Cover art by Christine Peterkin: e-mail@christinepeterkin.ca

To order additional copies, visit:
www.essencebookstore.com

Guardian Books is an imprint of *Essence Publishing,* a Christian Book Publisher dedicated to furthering the work of Christ through the written word. For more information, contact:
20 Hanna Court, Belleville, Ontario, Canada K8P 5J2
Phone: 1-800-238-6376 • Fax: (613) 962-3055
Email: info@essence-publishing.com
Web site: www.essence-publishing.com

I see such beauty there,
No other can compare,
I worship Thee, my Lord,
Within the veil.

Turn Your Eyes Upon Jesus

Turn your eyes upon Jesus
Look full in His wonderful face.
And the things of earth will grow strangely dim
In the light of His glory and grace.

He Is So Beautiful

He is so beautiful, Just look upon Him;
He is so beautiful, Heaven's diadem;
He is so beautiful, Behold Him and see
The beauty of Jesus, Heaven's majesty.

In Your Presence

In Your presence, In Your presence, There is peace.
In Your presence, In Your presence, There is joy.
I will linger, I will stay
In Your presence day by day,
That Your likeness
May be seen in me.

I Want To Worship the Lord

I want to worship the Lord
With all my heart,
Give Him my all, and not just a part.
Lift up my hands to The King of kings,
And praise Him in everything.

DEDICATED TO:

The wonderful memory of my parents
who gave so much and got so little,
who demonstrated the true value of being a Christian.

To my beautiful wife and daughters and son-in-law
for their patience and correction, enduring all things
in helping to bring this book to you.

To my wonderful church family
who pray for me continuously.

And most of all to the work of my gracious Lord and Saviour,
Jesus Christ, for without Him there is no book
and there is no voice.

Let the Lord speak and let the Church rejoice,
for the presence of the Lord is in the house.
I am so blessed because I heard the voice of the Lord.
You can too.

Table of Contents

Preface

Welcome to *It's All About Jesus*. As we begin to read this book, I'd like you to consider making this a time of worship. I would like us to just spend a few moments in an intimate way with Him.

When I come before the Lord, I begin by saying the Disciples' Prayer, and then I sing some of the beautiful choruses I learned over the years. It seems the presence of God is manifested as we commune together. You can add your own songs, but there is a continuous flow here and a message to be gleaned. I do not own the rights to any of these songs but I love to sing them. If you do not know the words or melodies, you can find them on the internet. It's worth the search.

THE DISCIPLES' PRAYER/THE LORD'S PRAYER

Our Father who art in heaven,
Hallowed be thy name.
Thy Kingdom come,
Thy will be done,
On earth as it is in heaven.
Give us this day our daily bread;
And forgive us our trespasses,
As we forgive those who trespass against us.
And lead us not into temptation,
But deliver us from evil: For thine is the Kingdom,
And the power, and the glory,
For ever and ever.
Amen.
(Matthew 6:9-13)

CHORUSES

There's Just Something About That Name

Jesus, Jesus, Jesus; there's just something about that name.
Master, Savior, Jesus, like the fragrance after the rain;
Jesus, Jesus, Jesus, let all Heaven and earth proclaim
Kings and kingdoms will all pass away,
But there's something about that name.
Kings and kingdoms will all pass away,
But there's something about that name.

Within the Veil

Within the veil I now would come,
Into the holy place
To look upon Thy face.

Church, As We Know It, is Over

T he Church, like everything else in the world is changing. The question is, are we willing to allow the LORD TO CHANGE US in order to be more relevant. The Church is at a major crossroads in her multi-millennial sojourn through time upon this earth. People that God has called to manage things have some big decisions to make. Most have no idea of the changes that are in the wind.

I remember when the Lord called me into the ministry. The Scripture He gave me as my mandate was Matthew 10:7-8: *"As you go, preach, saying, 'The kingdom of heaven is at hand'"* (NKJV, emphasis mine). I thought, "What does this mean?" Verse 8 says, "heal the sick, cleanse the lepers, raise the dead, cast out devils: freely you have received, freely give." My thoughts—wrong guy. No can do. This went on for quite a while. One day I asked, "Where do I go to tell this and to whom?" The Lord said, "The lost sheep of the house of Israel. Not just to tell but to do."

Before I came into the ministry, I was in construction. Some of the things our company did was build Ontario Place, The Metro Toronto Zoo, and Canada's Wonderland. I was one of the many supervisors on these projects. We were all very proud of our accomplishments. The Lord reminded me of these things, and He also said He wanted me to work with Him in building His Church. This will be the biggest thing ever. The Lord went on to say that the Church was not a physical but a spiritual temple. "I will build My Church and the gates of hell will not affect it," He said (Matthew 16:18). This house is going to be built with lively stones; it is a spiritual house. (1 Peter 2:5) Jesus, Himself will be the chief cornerstone. It will be a house where God Himself would live by His Spirit, doing Holy Spirit of God things, through human beings (verse 9) and so on. This is a great chapter in the Bible.

Then He said this to me: "My Church is not an entertainment centre. It is not a place for new themes to be pitched, nor is it a zoo. It is a place where people's lives will be changed; they will become new creatures, nothing like they were before.

"If you will work with Me, I will lead you, show you, and teach you. I will never leave you to figure it out by yourself." For forty-one years, I have been learning about this and the Lord has been telling me, "It's time to get to work to put into action the things I have shown you."

Much of the Church as we know it today celebrates Easter with pageantry and form, telling the story of our Lord's Crucifixion, death, burial, and resurrection and that seems to be it. I am all for keeping these memories alive and we are encouraged to do this—to tell our children and grandchildren in order to keep the memories alive. But, I think it is supposed to mean much more than that.

I think of the children of Israel gathering by the side of the Jordan River looking over at the Promised Land and wondering what it would be like. I feel like preaching here but I must go on.

The Charismatics, the Pentecostals, and the Revivalists are all crowded by the side of the Jordan wondering what it would be like. The Holy Spirit is urging them, calling, and trying to lead them across, but few will be able to go. Why? Because religious folks will not want to risk what they have inherited from their ancestors and built onto themselves. They will preach great sermons on what they think the kingdom of God is like, ever learning, but never really coming to a true knowledge of what the kingdom is all about. Few will admit they have lost the faith, the daring adventure of walking with the Lord and seeing as well as experiencing the manifest presence of God. Denominationalism is an anathema to them. Their attitude is we must protect what have or we have nothing.

But those who choose not to cross the river will not change the world. They do not rock the boat; neither will they see anything new, or experience anything deeper than what they have already felt and "telt."

God does have a destination for His Church and He is looking for builders to work with Him. He wants to manifest His love, compassion, and power, which is what Jesus came to do.

If He had not been raised from the grave on the first Easter Sunday, we would not be here today. The Church, as we know it today, has asked God for wealth, when He has wanted to give us nations; we have focused on getting healed, when He has wanted to make us healers. We continue to search for mercy and compassion, when He has called us to be distributors of these treasures to a dying and lost world. We are self-examining, when He wants us to be poured out to others as drink offerings to the thirsty, and to be bread to the hungry.

You may not like what I am about to tell you next, but here it is. The self-centered, needs-oriented, program-driven, dream-killing counterfeit is about to be replaced by the real Church of Jesus Christ.

It is not a zoo, a theme park, or an entertainment centre. It is a life-giving, hell-defeating, healing of sickness, blind eyes seeing, deaf people hearing, dumb speaking, lame walking, dead coming back to life message coming from a group of people who are drawn together by the chords of love—a Christ-centred, Kingdom-declaring, light-shining people who are the very heartthrob of God Himself.

They are a people who hear His voice and respond with joy and excitement, not fear and uncertainty. A life-giving, God-honouring group of worshippers whose greatest joy is hearing His voice. This Church understands that the hands Jesus stretches out to heal will be our hands. They know the hug they give is from Jesus; the smile, the encouragement, the world's only hope and glory is Jesus expressed through His people. It is very clear. This is the Church Jesus is building.

Please don't fight the changes God wants to bring into your life. He is changing you from glory to glory. God has pushed the big red reset button. It is time to ask hard questions. "What would You have me do, Lord?" Thank God for the Charismatic movement as we know it. But now, it is over and we must move on.

A new generation Church is emerging. New paradigms are developing relationships, not just with one another, but with other churches. No labels, only love. We are facing an unprecedented global opportunity for evangelism. For example, look at how we are having Church today. Me, here on Facebook—keeping in mind that we are not to forget the assembling together of ourselves one to another. Oh, what will it be like when this Covid-19 pandemic is over? We will be like the folks of old who said, "I was glad when they said unto me, let us go up to the house of the Lord." It will be good to get together again, but it will be different. Amen.

CHAPTER 1

We Welcome You, Holy Spirit

Just as Jesus had promised, the Holy Spirit came. This, we know today as Pentecost. According to our Scriptures, in Acts 2:1-4, Pentecost is a day. Pentecost is a dispensation. Pentecost is a delight. Pentecost was foretold. Pentecost was fulfilled, and Pentecost is for the Church. The Holy Spirit ministers in the Church, for the Church, and through the Church. In Acts 13, we see how the Holy Spirit ministered in the Church. In verse 2, the Holy Spirit spoke, the Holy Spirit separated, and in verse 3, the Holy Spirit sent. Jesus told His disciples about the work of the Holy Spirit in the Church in John 16:7-15:

"Nevertheless I tell you the truth; it is expedient for you that I go away: for if I do not go away, the Comforter will not come unto you; but if I depart, I will send him unto you. And when he is come, he will reprove the world of sin, and of righteousness, and of judgment: Of sin, because they believe not on me; of righteousness,

because I go to my Father, and ye see me no more; of judgment, because the prince of this world is judged. I have yet many things to say unto you, but ye cannot bear them now. Howbeit when he, the Spirit of truth, is come, he will guide you into all truth: for he shall not speak of himself; but whatsoever he shall hear, that shall he speak: and he will shew you things to come. He shall glorify me: for he shall receive of mine, and shall shew it unto you. All things that the Father hath are mine: therefore said I, that he shall take of mine, and shall shew it unto you."

No longer will the things of God be hidden from those that seek Him. The dwelling place of God is not a building made by hands from wood or stone; but the dwelling place of God is in the Church. We are the people of God who have submitted our lives to Christ and have become the dwelling place of God. The throne of God is upon our hearts and this is where God rules from by His Spirit. First of all, God speaks to us as individuals; He reveals Himself to us. Jesus said, "My sheep know My voice; another they will not follow." The gospel we have received through Jesus is not hidden; it is revealed to us and through us.

This is not nearly as complicated as some people would like to make it. We should not have any trouble talking about what is real and what is not real. Back in the second century, Justin Martyr said this: "If you want to prove that the Spirit of God has left you, come to our assemblies, and there you shall see Him casting out devils and healing the sick and He will speak with other tongues and prophecy."

In the third century, Tertullian joined the Montanists because the gift of prophecy was practiced among them.

In the fourth and fifth centuries, in the Celtic Church of Scotland, Ireland, and Wales, gifts of the Holy Spirit were operating.

God gave some gracious revivals in southern Europe—one was among the Waldenses, in which people spoke in other tongues; some revivals are recorded in the seventeenth century—the Huguenots in France, and Martin Luther's Reformation; in the 18th century there were revivals led by John Wesley, George Whitefield, Howell Harris, and Charles Finney; and in the 20th century, many thousands of people received the Holy Spirit and spoke in tongues around the world. We have many records of the manifestation of the Holy Spirit revealing the Lord Jesus Christ to us in our present dispensation.

The Lord has told us on numerous occasions that He would pour out His Spirit upon all flesh in the last days. There is no limit to the Holy Spirit; there are no barriers to the Holy Spirit for all those who are born again—the glorious super-abundance of the Holy Spirit fulfilling the promises of God to all who will believe. God gives the Holy Spirit to those who obey Him. The Holy Spirit is not just a word. The Holy Spirit is a member of the Godhead—the Trinity—and we must understand that, in order to understand God's method of revealing Himself to mankind.

One of the great gifts of the Holy Spirit is the prophetic gift—God speaking through human vessels to other humans, things that are divine. He will show us things to come. He will help us to understand things that are, and He will give us power to do the things He asked us to do.

We must understand that God's purpose in the Church is to reveal Himself in such a way that people will come to

Him, ask for forgiveness for their sin, and accept eternal life with Him. The Bible tells us that Jesus came to give us life, life that is more abundant. He did not come to give us another ideology. He came to give us life, a life like He had. He knew, and we need to know, that everybody that has not accepted the Lord Jesus Christ as their Saviour is lost. We are missionaries or, we could be called "ambassadors of heaven." God has commissioned us to preach the gospel to every creature. He has given us the Holy Spirit to enable us to do that; we are to seek and to save those who are lost, just like Jesus did.

There are three things that stand out in the Book of Acts, that we need to be very aware of: 1) The disciples were mightily anointed with the Holy Spirit to win souls; 2) The Holy Spirit gave them power and grace to suffer persecution; 3) The Holy Spirit empowered them to heal the sick.

The Holy Spirit has nine major gifts by which He does His work—the word of wisdom, the word of knowledge, faith, healing, working of miracles, prophecy, discerning of spirits, diverse kinds of tongues, and the interpretation of tongues. The Holy Spirit also equips people whom God calls to do special things in His name. He calls some apostles, some prophets, some evangelists, and some pastors and teachers. Through these special gifts of the Holy Spirit, God brings the whole Church into the unity of the faith, whereby He may cleanse it and empower it to do the work of heaven here on earth. The Church of Jesus Christ is to be a glorious manifestation of the Lord Jesus Christ. We must understand that our responsibility in serving God is to bring an awareness of who Jesus Christ is, what He came to earth for, what He did, and what He is doing.

This can only be accomplished as the Holy Spirit is accepted and allowed to function as God has determined. It's the Holy Spirit's job to bring the Church to perfection and, as He is allowed to function, He will do this. God said to Abram, in Genesis, "Walk before Me and be thou perfect." In Matthew, Jesus said, "Do this, even as our Father in heaven is perfect," and Paul said, "Be perfect, be of good comfort, be of one mind, live in peace; and the God of love and peace shall be with you."

It is interesting that we are made from dust, and now, because of the infilling of the Holy Spirit, "Dust shall have dominion." This is amazing! The Holy Spirit has come to convict the sinner of his sin and to show him there is a better way; and that better way is the life Jesus came and gave to us. John tells us, "As many as received Him, to them He gave power to become the sons of God." The Holy Spirit working within us will demonstrate God in us. The Spirit of God will bear witness to our spirit that we are God's children.

The Holy Spirit has also been given to teach us God's Word, and how to live according to it, through the many gifts and administrations we have previously mentioned. The Holy Spirit will give to each and every one of us, grace, joy, and liberty, in our moment of need. We need to live the life that Jesus has promised us. The Holy Spirit comes to live within us, as the Scriptures tell us—the very God of peace will sanctify you holy, and preserve you, spirit, soul, and body that we may be blameless when the Lord comes to receive us.

So while we are here on earth, as the Holy Spirit lives and abides within us, we can demonstrate the fruit of the Spirit—love, joy, peace, long-suffering, gentleness, goodness, faith, meekness, and temperance. We are not alone; God is with us. The Holy Spirit has been given to abide within us, to quicken us in resurrection power and glory, so that we may be fashioned like unto Christ—that glorious Body, the Church.

The activity of the Holy Spirit can be found on every page in the book of Acts, which is an autobiography of the Holy Spirit. He pioneers the progress of the Church. He becomes the authority in shaping the doctrine of the Church. He appoints and allocates the callings and ministries in the Church. He sets up the Church government with Jesus Christ as its head. He does not speak of Himself—He speaks of Jesus. He glorifies Jesus. That is His total purpose in this present age. The Holy Spirit overshadowed Jesus Christ at His birth, led Him into the wilderness and out again in power, raised Jesus from the dead, and presented Him for inspection, to our senses—we have seen, we have heard, and we have handled the Lord Jesus Christ.

The Holy Spirit today is the administrator of the Church of what is going on in heaven. When we ask the Heavenly Father, in prayer, to do here on earth what is being done in heaven, it is the Holy Spirit's responsibility to bring that to pass within us. He has the power to speak on God's behalf; He has the power to heal; He has the power to cast out devils; He has the power to witness; and He has the power to defeat any and all principalities or powers that would try to exalt themselves against God.

How does this work? The Holy Spirit lives in human beings. John 14:17 states, *"He dwells with you and shall be in you"* (NKJV). In Romans 8:9, we read, *"The Spirit of God dwells in you"* (NKJV). The coming of the Holy Spirit brought the end of the old dispensation of the Law, and began a new dispensation called grace. No longer is the Holy Spirit limited to an individual; He permeates the entire Church. He challenges the Church to a vocation of holiness, to produce a divine character called "Christ-like-ness." The Church is God's fullest and final revelation of Himself, and is the greatest entity on earth.

The apostle Paul said this, "Our gospel has not come to you in word only, but also in power, through the Holy Spirit." The Gospel is contained and translated by the vehicle of words; they are not empty words; they are words that are taken, not touched, and transfused and transfigured by the Holy Spirit. When Peter preached, they were words of power, rich and vitalized by a vocabulary endowed by the Spirit, words which the Holy Spirit gave. The Holy Spirit still gives the Church those same words of power today. Because the Holy Spirit lives within us, we can experience the life of Christ within ourselves. This is why we should be able to pray and say, "In the name of Jesus"—words, with power provided by the Holy Spirit.

The Holy Spirit on earth is the mouthpiece of the Trinity in counsel. The Holy Spirit's disbursement of revelation spontaneously translates the mind of the unseen God. The Holy Spirit decodes for us the legacy of God's will drawn up from the eternal ages. So, therefore, we should take heed unto ourselves and to all the flock over which the Holy Spirit has made us overseers, to feed the Church of God which Jesus purchased with His own blood.

In this chapter I tried to demonstrate who the Holy Spirit is, and why it is so important to us that we understand Him completely. I believe many people, both inside and outside of the Church today, suffer needlessly because they do not realize the Church is here and available to meet their every need. The sinner should be able to find salvation in the Church. The saint should be able to find healing, deliverance, protection from the evil one, hope, and strength to fulfill God's purpose and calling in their life. The Holy Spirit is here to comfort and equip the Church, and prepare it for the coming of the Lord. We are in the last days of this dispensation of grace; we do not need to live in misery and suffering. It does not have to be that way; Jesus is the answer to all our needs. The Holy Spirit has been sent to us to reveal Jesus to us, so that we might come to Him and allow Him to not only be our Saviour, but to be Lord of our lives. Thank You for coming, precious Holy Spirit.

CHAPTER 2

It is All About Jesus, Our Saviour and Lord!

n trying to understand who the Lord Jesus Christ is, I believe that one of the first places in the Word of God that we can go to for this, is the Book of Revelation.

For many of the people I talked to, the Book of Revelation is a book of questions; to some, it is a book of fear; and, to others, it is a book of glory. It is a book of non-concealment. If we only see the Beast, the tribulations, and the Whore of Babylon, we could miss the whole thing.

The opening sentence in the Book should give us a clear clue as to what we will find—"The Revelation of the Lord Jesus Christ."

It is an uncovering.

- A mystery understood.
- A question answered.
- A way explained.
- A mountain removed.
- A light in the dark.

- A river in a desert.
- Life in place of death.

The Book of Revelation is the final Word in the divine library of God, giving us a panoramic picture of what the great story in the Bible is all about—Jesus.

Without this story in the Book of Revelation, we would have a great story with no ending, a prophecy without a prophet, a messenger without a message; this Book is what makes being a Christian different from all other types of religion.

Everything commenced in all the other parts of Scripture, find their conclusion in the Book of Revelation. In Genesis, you will find the commencement of heaven and earth; but in Revelation, you will find the consummation. In Genesis, you will see the dawn of Satan and his activity; but in Revelation, we see the doom of Satan and his activity. In Genesis, we see the entrance of sin and the curse; but in Revelation, we find the exit of sin and the curse. In Genesis, the Tree of Life is relinquished; but in Revelation, the Tree of Life is regained. In Genesis, death enters; and, in Revelation, death exits. In Genesis, sorrow has begun; but in Revelation, sorrow is banished.

This Book has been written to produce a sanctifying effect in the lives of humanity. Here we see heavenly and earthly activities; we see angels and demons warring in the heavens and in Armageddon, here on earth; we see the golden millennium (1000 year reign of the Lord); we also see the destruction of Satan; and, we see the creation of a new heaven and a new earth. Even though we read here about the Apocalypse, we need to understand that this just helps us to understand the revelation of the glory and majesty of our Saviour, the Lord Jesus Christ. We witness His radiance, His sovereign power, and His utmost dignity. The core of this message is to help us get our eyes off our circumstances and get our eyes upon the Lord. We need to understand that Jesus Christ is not only alive, but He is glorified by God and He knows you. He has proven to all, so that we may see through the words of this Book, if we would hear His voice and obey it, our hope would rise, our faith would come alive, and the darkness of our souls would disappear. The reason we can so adamantly declare this, is because He is risen from the dead and He is alive for evermore. So let us now look into this Book to see why it is all about Jesus, our Lord and Saviour.

First of all, let us look at the subject of Revelation. Here, the curtain is pulled back, and we are now allowed to see Jesus Christ in His glory and majesty. The veil has truly been pulled back. This may appear to be a little different than what we are used to seeing in the Gospels; there, we do not see all the glory of Christ in His total regal splendor. Mostly, we see His human side or the humiliation of Christ. He is fully God, but His glory is covered over because of His humanity. We see a suffering servant, One who was crucified for our sins and was humiliated that we might be liberated. He was born in poverty and obscurity. He knew what it was to hunger and thirst. He was beaten, buffeted, and bruised. He was plunged into the depths of agony. He died in ignominy. For the most part, this is what the Gospels tell us. We do see glimpses of His glory as we read in John 17:1, where Jesus is talking to the Father about His departure and His glorification to come: *"Glorify thy Son, that thy Son also may glorify thee."*

So now, in the Gospels, before we come to Revelation, we see glimpses of His glory—on the Mount of Transfiguration, where Jesus outshines the noonday sun; when He walked up to the tomb of Lazarus, who had been dead for three days, his body already decaying, and called him out—a dead man came to life at the command of the Lord Jesus; when Jesus walked into the bedroom of a dead twelve-year-old girl and spoke to her in the language she could not hear, saying, "Damsel, I say unto you arise," and she got up; and, again, when Jesus, walking into a village called Nain, saw a funeral procession moving through the city gates and, looking at the young man in the coffin, told him to rise. He got up out of the coffin, and his mother and all those around were very happy. This is another glimpse of the glory of Jesus.

As much as the Gospels declare the humiliation of the Lord, the Book of Revelation declares the glorification of our Lord.

- In the Gospels, Jesus receives death; in Revelation, He is revered.

- In the Gospels, Jesus comes to convict; but, in Revelation, He comes to judge.

- In the Gospels, His enemies applaud; but, in Revelation, His enemies appeal.

- In the Gospels, we see Him in His misery; but, in Revelation, we see Him in Majesty.

- In the Gospels, Jesus is the Saviour; but, in Revelation, He is the Intercessor.

- In the Gospels, Jesus is pierced; but, in Revelation, He is praised.

- In the Gospels, He appears as a victim; but, in Revelation, He is the victor.
- In the Gospels, they crowned Him with thorns; in Revelation, He is seated on the throne.
- In the Gospels, Jesus is hung on a cross; but, in Revelation, He is crowned.
- In the Gospels, they called Him a criminal; but, in Revelation, He is the conquering King.
- In the Gospels, Jesus accepted our guilt; but, in Revelation, He receives glory.

In the book of Revelation, we see Jesus being glorified by the Father. He is risen from the dead, full of power and splendour, totally righteous, and absolutely holy; He is the Lord Jesus, the Christ. He is never again to be spat upon, never again to be robed in misery, never again to wear a crown of thorns. I believe that we could say, "We have seen the Lord." The lives of everyone in Scripture who saw the Lord, were changed.

So, let us ask a few of the people from the Bible about their experience in meeting the Lord.

"Isaiah, did you see the glory of the Lord Jesus Christ? What happened when you saw Him?" "When I saw His glory, I shouted, 'Woe is me, for I am undone.'"

If we could ask Peter, "Did you see the Lord's glory?" Peter might say to us, "Get away from me, for I am a sinful man." If we were to ask John, "Did you see the Lord's glory?" John may respond by saying, "I sure did, and I fell at His feet as though dead."

"Job, did you see the Lord's glory?" "Yes, I did, and I repented in sackcloth and ashes." "Paul, did you see the glory of the Lord Jesus Christ?" "Yes. I was traveling down the road to a city called Damascus when suddenly I saw a great light that was brighter than the noonday sun and, for the next few days, I was blinded by the glory of the Lord Jesus Christ." Thus, a glimpse of God's glory turned a murderer into an Apostle. The question we need to ponder at this time is, "Have we seen the glory of the Lord?" If not, maybe we may see His glory revealed in this Book of Revelation.

The second thing I would like to look at is the significance of the Book of Revelation.

Keep in mind that the apostle John wrote this book during the time of the Roman emperor, Domitian. That was a very calamitous time for the Christian Church. Christianity was the target of harrassment by all the other world religions. There were terrible consequences for being a believer in Christ. Domitian had set himself up as God and demanded that the Christians worship him. (It seems as though history may be repeating itself in our day.) They needed a message of hope, so God spoke to John to fortify them. Persecution was coming upon them with hurricane force. The days of life were not very gentle. They used to seem very nice, but now were very dark. Hopes were being diminished, dreams were being shattered, and their dignity was being taken by the storms of disappointment. There were raids throughout their ranks, the winds of disaster were blowing and, emotionally, they were ripped to shreds. They went into a place of sorrow and felt every pain. John was one of those Christians and, here, in this dark cave on the Island of Patmos, God gives him a great message of hope: "Take your eyes off your circumstances and begin to focus upon Jesus." I believe John was very close to the Lord at this point in his life. Sometimes, in our darkest hours, we can get our greatest revelation. Remember, your life is hidden with Christ in God.

John was able to take his eyes off his circumstances and the world around him, and turn what appeared to be a tragedy into triumph. As we look around the world we live in today, we can see where Christian values and principles seem to mean very little to a lot of people; but, I believe, if we can see Jesus in this Book of Revelation, our hearts may be encouraged, as was John's and, like him, we might be able to tell the story of having seen the Lord Jesus.

In Psalm 121, it is written:

"I will lift up mine eyes unto the hills, from whence cometh my help. My help cometh from the Lord, which made heaven and earth. He will not suffer thy foot to be moved: he that keepeth thee will not slumber...nor sleep. The Lord is thy keeper: the Lord is thy shade upon thy right hand. The sun shall not smite thee by day, nor the moon by night. The Lord shall preserve thee from all evil: he shall preserve thy soul. The Lord shall preserve thy going out and thy coming in from this time forth, and even for evermore."

Psalm 68:5 tells us, *"A father of the fatherless, and a judge of the widows, is God in his holy habitation."* Psalm 34:4 declares, *"I sought the Lord and he heard me and delivered me from all my fears."* In Matthew 14, we find Jesus walking on the water. He is above the storms of life. So what can we learn and what is significant to us today in seeing who Jesus, in Revelation, is all about? The things that are going on all around us do not have to be the things that control us, but if we can fix our eyes upon Jesus, our circumstances will change.

We are living in the world today where the suicide rate amongst our young people and the indigenous people in our country is the highest it has been in history. It is my conviction that if we, the Church, can show people who the Lord Jesus Christ is, from what we learn about Him in this Book of Revelation, life can change for these people. It does not have to remain this way; Jesus can make the change.

So why am I writing this book after all these years of walking with the Lord? Why is it important to try and write a book about my experience and who the Lord Jesus Christ is to me? My thoughts are along this line: "If something in my life can help somebody in theirs, all this will be worthwhile."

It is hard today to listen to the radio or television, or to pick up any kind of book or magazine and find something encouraging. The days we live in are very dark. By that I mean, sin abounds. The frightening part about this is that the wages of sin are still death and separation from God for eternity; but there is a gift from God which we cannot earn, that He freely gives us so that we may live with Him eternally. Yes, this way is very narrow and few there are that find it. My hope is that, if you read the Book of Revelation, you might find the way that leads to eternal life, get your eyes off your circumstances, and look unto Jesus, the author and finisher of your life. He created you; He has a plan for you; and He will help you fulfill that plan. It does not need to be all bad. Life is good when you know the Lord.

The Book of Revelation, as we said in the beginning, raises many questions but also provides many answers and tells us what is going to happen on this planet. We are in the last days. The terribleness, the trauma, the pain, and the suffering that this old world is going to experience does not need to be your experience.

I met a Jewish man. We used to go swimming at the same club a couple of times a week. He would always try to somehow say something negative about my Christianity. Being a good Christian, I thought, "I will never ever argue with him and I will let him talk and, then, maybe just give a little thought and leave it at that." One day, an off day for me, he said something that irritated me. I said to him in a frustrated way, "What's the matter with you? You Jews have had Jesus all of your life and you still haven't figured out who He is? When you go home, if you have a Bible, look up Isaiah 9 and read it. Maybe you might understand who Jesus is." He did not say anything more to me. That was the end of our conversation that day. I went home and did not think I had represented my Lord very well. So I repented and it seemed to disappear from me and everything seemed to be fine.

I did not meet my friend at the pool for a couple of months, and I began to wonder if he was sick or if something had happened. One day, I went into McDonald's for a coffee and he was sitting there with his wife. When he saw me, he proudly stood up and showed me the necklace he was wearing with the Star of David. I looked at it and said, "That's very nice." He said, "Take another look." I did, and I noticed it also contained a cross. I looked at it for a moment and then, I looked up into his face and my friend was weeping. He said, "I call you Mr. Isaiah." "Why do you do that?" I asked. He said, "I went home that day and looked up in the Bible what you told me. My wife and I went to the Baptist Church the next Sunday and gave our hearts to the Lord. I don't know how I can ever thank you for being so mean to me." We laughed and, of course, had a small celebration at McDonald's, but what a wonderful feeling it was. Before leaving, I told him that Jesus was in every book of the Bible, and he said he could hardly wait for me to show him where to find Him.

As I did for this gentleman, I want to take the time today to show you. In Genesis, Jesus is the seed of the woman; in Exodus, He is the Passover Lamb. In Leviticus, He is the High Priest; in Numbers, He is the pillar of cloud by day and the pillar of fire by night. In Deuteronomy, He is the prophet, just like Moses. In Joshua, He is there as the Captain of our salvation, and, in Judges, He is the Judge and Lawgiver. In Ruth, He is the kinsman Redeemer; in Samuel, He is the trusted prophet. In Kings and Chronicles, He is the reigning King. In Ezra, Jesus is our faithful scribe; in Nehemiah, He is the builder of the broken down walls of our lives. In Esther, He is our Mordecai; in Job, Jesus is our dayspring. In the Psalms, Jesus is the Lord our Shepherd, and in Proverbs and Ecclesiastes, He is our wisdom. In the Song of Solomon, He is our love and our bridegroom. He is everywhere.

The Bible tells us in Isaiah that Jesus is our Prince of Peace; Jeremiah tells us He is the Righteous Branch. In Lamentations, He is the weeping prophet; in Ezekiel, He is the wheel that is turning. In Daniel, you see Him in the fiery furnace; in Hosea, He is the bridegroom married to the backslider. In Joel, He is the baptizer with the Holy Spirit. In Amos, He is the burden bearer; in Obadiah, He is the mighty Saviour and, in Jonah, He is that great foreign missionary. In Micah, He is the messenger with the beautiful feet carrying the Gospel. In Nahum, He is the avenger of God elect; in Habakkuk, He is that great evangelist, prime for revival. In Zephaniah, He is the restorer of God's lost heritage. In Haggai, He is a cleansing fountain; in the book of Zechariah, He is the merciful father and, in Malachi, He is the Son of Righteousness rising with healing in His wings. Yes, Jesus is everywhere in the Bible and on every page.

Now, let's look at the New Testament. Matthew said, Jesus is the Messiah. Mark said, He is a miracle worker. Luke said, He is the Son of Man, and John declared Him the Son of God. In Chapter 15, John also said: He is the vine, He is the tree of life, the river, the mountain, the plain, the valley, the shade, the light, the strength and the comfort, the helper who heals. He is the door, He is the way, the truth, and the life. He is my everything, He is my all. In the book of Acts, they all declared, "He is the ascended Lord;" in Romans, Paul calls Him the Justifier. In Corinthians, He is the motivator of the Spirit. In Galatians, He is the One who sets us free. In Ephesians, the Bible tells us He is the Christ of riches; in Philippians, He is the God who meets our every need. In Colossians, He's the fullness of the Godhead who dwells bodily in mankind. In Thessalonians, He is the soon coming King; in Timothy, He is the mediator between God and man. In Titus, He is a faithful pastor; and, in the book of Hebrews, He is the blood who washes our sins away. In James, He is the Great Physician; in Peter, He is the Chief Shepherd. In John, He is the everlasting love; in Jude, He is the Lord coming down with ten thousands of His saints. And in Revelation, He is the King of kings and the Lord of lords. He is all in all; He is everywhere, He is everlasting, He is everything to all men everywhere. He is Jesus.

The One that John sees in Revelation is not dead; He is alive. In Revelation 5:6, He (Jesus) is standing as a Lamb having been slain; and here we are today casting crowns before Him, crying: "Worthy, worthy is the Lamb; Worthy is the Lamb to receive honour, and power, and glory!" Here, in this Book of Revelation, is the mystery revealed, the One who is the Christ.

The last thing I want to point out is that the symbolism of Christ the Messiah is found in the Old Testament; and, the revelation concerning Christ Jesus, is found in the New Testament—in the Old Testament a sign is given which is fulfilled in the New Testament, as follows: Genesis 3:15 gives the sign that Jesus Christ truly had to be the seed of the woman; in Galatians 4:4 we see that sign was fulfilled. Genesis 12:3 gives the sign that He must be the seed of Abraham; in Matthew 1:1 we see that Jesus is a descendant of Abraham. Genesis 17:19 says He must be the seed of Isaac; Luke 3:34 says that Jesus is a descendant of Isaac. Genesis 49:10 gives the sign that He must descend from the tribe of Judah; Luke 3:33 shows that Jesus is a descendant of Judah. Micah 5:2 says Jesus Christ must be born in Bethlehem; and in Luke 2:4 we read that Jesus was born in Bethlehem. Isaiah 7:14 says He must be born of a virgin; Luke 1:27, 31 tells us Mary, Jesus' mother, was a virgin. Hosea 11:1 gives the sign that He will be called out of Egypt; in Matthew 2:13-15, we read that Jesus and His parents flee to Egypt (later returning to live in Nazareth). Psalm 78:2 says He must come speaking in parables; Matthew 13:34 tells us Jesus spoke to the multitudes in parables.

Isaiah 61:1-2 gives the sign that He must heal the brokenhearted; in Luke 4:18, Jesus said He was sent to heal the broken-hearted. Isaiah 53:3 gives the sign that He will be rejected by His own people; in John 1:11 we read that He came to His own but His own received Him not. Isaiah 53:7 says He will be silent as He stands before those who accuse Him; and in Mark 15:5, we read that He stood before Pilate and opened not His mouth. Psalm 22:1, says He shall be forsaken by God, the Father; and in Matthew 27:46, Jesus cried from the cross, "ELI ELI LAMA SABACHTHANI?—My God, My God why have You forsaken me?" It happened. Isaiah 53:9 gives the sign that He will be buried with the rich; Matthew 27:57-60 tells us Jesus was buried with the rich. (The devil thought he had Jesus where he wanted Him—dead in the tomb, but Jesus was about to crash his party.) Psalm 49:15 gives the sign that there will be a resurrection—Jesus would get up from the grave; Mark 16:6 tells us "He is not here, He is risen. Come and see the place where He lay for He is not here."

Jesus is in every book of the Bible. He is on every page in the Bible and the Bible is what Jesus is all about.

CHAPTER 3

The God Who Hides Himself

This to me has become one of the greatest things I have ever discovered. How is it possible for the God of Creation to be hidden from that which He has created? It has been a puzzle I believe, not just to myself, but to many who seek an understanding and a knowledge of where we are and where we came from. Isaiah states, "Thou art a God who hides Himself, O God of Israel, the Saviour." In Job 23:8-9 we read, *"I go forward, but he is not there; and backward, but I cannot perceive him: on the left hand...but I cannot behold him: he hideth himself on the right hand, that I cannot see him."*

You hide Yourself in the heavens; behold the heavens, and the heavens of evidence cannot contain You. You not only dwell in eternity, but eternity dwells in me. It is amazing to know that He who created and sustained all things by the word of His power stays hidden, despite the fact that You are omniscient—You know everything; You are omnipotent—there is no limit to Your power. You are omnipresent—You are everywhere. You are totally sovereign in both the material realm and in the angelic realm as well. Your greatness, O God is unsearchable.

You came to Your own and they did not receive You; You came in Creation, You came in the prophetic, You came in judgment, You came in Kingship; yet the Word says You stood among them and they did not know You.

Jesus, on one occasion, told the people that He had come to them, yet they did not know who He was, because they did not know who His Father was; in other words, if you knew God, My Father, you would also know Me. You talk of the great wonderful works that I did for you down through the ages. You have the records of the great and mighty things that I have done; yet you do not know Me. You are rulers in Israel, yet you are ignorant of all I am. I am known by My righteous acts, yet you are determined to establish your own righteousness and self-righteousness, trusting in your own works, and this has brought you to spiritual ignorance. Your understanding of Me is darkened because you have alienated Me through your ignorance. You despised My Word, the Word of the Lord. Zechariah said, you made your hearts as hard as stone and you would not hear the words of the prophet.

The wisdom of God is hidden in all of Creation; the God who has hidden Himself, when looked for, will be revealed to those that are searching by the Holy Spirit. Yes, God is hidden in Creation; He is hidden in the Word; and He is hidden in His Son, the Lord Jesus.

I believe that God has revealed Himself, and this is why I want to write this book. I believe that these are some of the things the devil has used to deceive the people of God:

- Do not believe in the Trinity.
- We are not all born in sin. We are all God's children.
- Just believe; no repentance, no conversion, no holiness; infant baptism, confirmation, church membership—that's all you need to get into heaven.
- There are many ways that you can get to heaven.
- God is female.
- No virgin birth, no sinless life, no atoning death; the resurrection is questionable; He did not die; it was just an illusion.
- Justification and sanctification of the believer through the finished work of Christ is not sufficient; you must work for your salvation.
- The Baptism of the Holy Spirit for believers, with signs following, is not for today. It's only for the first century Christians.
- The message of faith is not to be believed.
- The Bible is full of errors and mistakes, therefore, it cannot be the inspired Word and authority of God.
- Do not believe that God gives visions and dreams to His people; those things are nightmares, hallucinations, and make-believe.
- Do not waste time confessing God's promises for your needs and putting God in remembrance of His Word.
- Do not preach and believe deliverance from demonic powers.
- Do not believe in the prophetic message of God's Word, whether it be from yesterday, or today, concerning tomorrow.

- Do not talk about repentance and turning from sin, as this is very difficult for people to understand.

These are some of the lies the devil is perpetrating today throughout mankind, to keep God's Creation, including us humans, from coming into harmony with God Himself. The devil will continue to say, "Can you see Him? Maybe He doesn't exist." The Bible warns us about these things. The thief cometh not but to steal, to kill, and to destroy. Do not give place to the devil. He is a Word stealer.

When the Word of God is not received, or is despised, or made light of, condemnation is the end result. God sends them—the people who are teaching these false doctrines—strong delusions, and those that believe these lies are afflicted with spiritual blindness, because unbelief is deceptive.

Jesus warns us to beware of these false teachers so that no man deceives us.

The God who hides Himself has a very special method that is seen and noticed. He calls it "revelation." All spiritual truths are matters of revelation, not discovery. Paul said the Gospel which was preached by him is "not after man, for I neither received it from man, nor was I taught it by man, but by revelation of Jesus Christ, Himself."

This revelation of Jesus Christ and the Church, as well as God Himself, has been hidden from the wise and the prudent and released to the humble and faithful to God. There are many methods of revelation: (1) Visions; (2) Prophetic visions; (3) the words of the Old Testament prophets; (4) the words of the New Testament prophets; (5) Creation; (6) the Lord Jesus Himself; (7) the Holy Spirit;

(8) through His holy apostles and prophets; (9) and now, through the Church.

There are four distinct revelations whereby God Himself will be revealed totally:

1. Revelation of God through Christ—through His life and ministry, His death, and resurrection.

2. The Revelation of God in the Church.

3. Revelation of God by the Holy Spirit.

4. The final Revelation of God will be in the coming again of the Lord Jesus Christ.

The Gospel of Jesus Christ still considered the unsearchable riches of Christ, which is that God was in Christ reconciling the world unto Himself. This mystery has been hidden from ages and generations in the past, but now is being made manifest to all the saints of God. Paul puts it like this: he said, "I pray that Christ be formed in you." He also said, "Christ in you is the hope of glory;" and he went on to say to the Philippians, "Rejoice in the knowledge that God is in you."

God was known in the Old Testament through His works and through His Law. He was never, ever really seen by man, yet man was used by God to do many wonderful things in Creation, through Creation, and for Creation. Again, in the midst of all that, God Himself was never seen.

Now we will move forward in our thoughts to Jesus. Jesus would make a statement like this one day to His disciples, "If you have seen Me, you have seen the Father." This raised a lot of questions for all the people that lived around there. Imagine, if you will, all the things that had taken place down through the ages of history and now, here is this one man standing up and declaring, "If you have seen Me, you have seen God."

He made other statements: "I only do what my Father tells Me. The works that I do are My Father's works. My Father and I are One; I am in Him and He is in Me. If you don't believe that, then believe the works that I do." Jesus did many miracles which were very similar to the things that God Himself had done back in the Old Testament. Because the people of that day had refused to believe the words of the prophets, they found it very difficult to believe that Jesus was the promised Messiah. Every Sabbath day in the synagogue, they would read the words declaring the coming of the Messiah yet, when He came, they refused to accept Him. God was manifested in the flesh. The Word was manifested in the flesh. There is absolutely no doubt in this great mystery, that God had enshrouded Himself in flesh to conceal His deity.

Therefore, it is only by revelation that we are able to see the greatness of God's eternal heart and purposes in the Church. On one occasion, when Jesus was talking to the woman at the well, He disclosed a very important fact. He said that God is a Spirit and they that worship Him must worship Him in spirit.

This now begins to unfold the great mystery of who God really is. It is very difficult for humanity to see a Spirit with the naked eye. I believe that this is one of the greatest understandings that we have, namely, that God is in all Creation. He is being magnified and glorified. God is in Christ. God is in the Church and, when we become born again, we are in God. This is truly a spiritual activity.

Our natural mind cannot comprehend the greatness of God—all He is and all He can do. It is difficult for the natural mind to comprehend that God could possibly live in a human being and still be God of the universe. This is why it is so important that we believe in the virgin birth, the sinless life, and the death and resurrection of our Lord and Saviour Jesus Christ. It could only be the power of God in Him that could bring Him back to life.

Now we can look at Creation and understand who God is. We can also look at the Lord Jesus and see who God is; but something still greater than all of this is yet to be revealed to all that God has created. So here we have it. Jesus has demonstrated who God is in Creation. He is no longer hidden; He revealed that God is in Jesus Himself and now He is revealed. Jesus, when He ascended from the earth, told the disciples, "I am going to send you the Holy Spirit." He is the third member of our Trinity. Not only has He revealed who God is in all of Creation, not only has He revealed who God is in Jesus, but when He comes, He is going to reveal who God is in you.

This even becomes more difficult for the human mind to comprehend. Jesus prayed in John 17:1, *"That they all may be one; as thou, Father, art in me, and I in thee, that they also may be one in us: that the world may believe that thou hast sent me."* In Acts 2, we read about the coming of the Holy Spirit—what it looks like, what we should expect, and how we will know it is Him. These are all questions I'm sure the early disciples had. It took them ten days in an upper room discussing this question. Exactly what they agreed on is not really spelled out, but it does say that when they all came into agreement, the Holy Spirit came, and when He came they knew it was Him. The reason they knew it was Him, is because He did things they saw Jesus do; and they saw Jesus do things that God had done; and because they were all similar, they knew it had to be the Holy Spirit.

Sad to say, many Christians today read these very words and do not understand them because, I believe, herein lies the revelation to the Church of who God really is. The God who hides Himself is about to make Himself known to those who believe in Him. The Holy Spirit begins to give out divine gifts to human people—gifts that allow human beings to execute and deliver the dynamic power and distribution of the mind and will of God. This can all be summed up in the words, "righteousness is being revealed."

For those of us who can look back into the Old Testament, we see that God was revealed in righteousness; we look into the New Testament and see that through the life of Jesus Christ, God was revealed through righteousness; and now we can believe that God is going to be revealed in the Church through righteousness. The revelation of the mystery of the Gospel of Jesus Christ, which was kept secret from the beginning of time, has now been revealed. Death has lost its sting, and the grave has lost its power; we live forever, because we are spirit. We will either live with God, Jesus, and the Holy Spirit, or we will live with Satan.

It is God's absolute will that who He is be revealed to humankind. The Word tells us, in Galatians 4, that in the fullness of time God sent forth His Son into the world to redeem those who were under the Law, that we might receive the adoption of sons; and, because we are considered sons, we will receive the same Spirit Jesus had—the Holy Spirit.

This is the mystery that has been hidden for ages; and now it has been revealed through the apostles and prophets, by the Holy Spirit, that the Gentiles should be fellow heirs of the same Body, and partakers of the promises of God through Christ in the Gospel. This means that the God who has hidden Himself through all the ages, is now made known, not only to the Jews, but also to the Gentiles. We are converted to Christ through repentance of our sins, and as a result of repenting, we can be forgiven. This means that we can call ourselves sons/daughters of God. We are heirs of God. Everything the Father had given to the Jews and to Jesus, has now been made available to the Gentiles. We are joint heirs with Jesus Christ and we can be glorified together with Him. Through the gift of repentance we are justified by God's grace, and we now have all eternity with Him. We are baptized in the Holy Spirit. This is the fulfillment of God's promise that He would come and live with us. Folks, this is all about Jesus—what He has done, and what He is doing.

Through Christ life on earth, death on the cross, resurrection from the dead, and ascension into heaven is now continuously make an intercession for us in heaven. God has now hidden Himself in our hearts by His Spirit. The God who has hidden Himself from the beginning of eternity, is now making Himself known to all mankind. Christ in us, is our hope for glory. Christ dwells in our hearts by faith. Now we can make this bold confession, "God has revealed Himself to me and in me. My God is real in my soul. I confess with my mouth and I believe in my heart that God has saved me. I can believe this very thing: that He who has begun this good work in me will perform it until the day Jesus comes back. I now believe that God will keep me, in this life, from falling into sin and losing my inheritance in God. Every day I can look out and see the heavens declare the glory of God, showing His handiwork in Creation. I believe in God because of the history of mankind—how God has undertaken, and gone to great lengths to preserve what He has created. It is Jesus who gave us the Gospel, which is, He came to take my sin or do away with my sin so that I would never have to face it again, and asked me only to believe that He did this. If I am willing to believe what He did was sufficient, I am saved." So now it is not just enough to be saved. We must tell others. The Bible tells us, that if this gospel is hidden it will be hidden from those who are lost. The God who was hidden from us in years past has now made Himself available to shine in our hearts, and remove the spiritual blindness, so that we may be one with Him.

Jesus made this declaration: "The works I have done while I was here with you on earth, are what My Father told Me to do and I did them. And in that My Father is revealed." Then Jesus went on to say, "I'm going to send you the Holy Spirit and you will be baptized by Him, and greater things than I have done you will do also. And as you do this, our heavenly Father and I will reveal ourselves to you and to others around you."

No longer is the God of Creation going to be hidden. God will reveal Himself to us by His Spirit. As I bring this chapter to a close, I want to leave these thoughts with you: One day the disciples saw Jesus praying—talking to His Father—and they said to Him, "Teach us how to pray like that;" so He did.

He said, "When you pray say, 'Our Father which art in heaven, Hallowed be Thy name. Thy Kingdom come. Thy will be done on earth as it is in heaven. Give us this day our daily bread. And forgive us our debts, as we forgive our debtors. And lead us not into temptation, but deliver us from evil; for Thine is the Kingdom and the power and the glory, forever. Amen.'"

The key thought here, is, "As it is in heaven so may it be on earth." It is my strong conviction that God, our heavenly Father, Jesus, our Lord and Saviour and, yes, brothers and sisters, the Holy Spirit, are managing the affairs of heaven in heaven. I also believe that those three—Father, Son, and Holy Spirit—are managing the affairs of earth here on earth just the way they are doing it in heaven. God is known, Jesus is known, and the Holy Spirit is known—no longer hidden, but revealed by the Spirit of God.

CHAPTER 4

Mixing Faith With the Gospel

As I continue sharing the things God has put on my heart, I would like to take you back to 1994, when I came to a point of burnout in the ministry. At this point, I had to step down from one of the greatest things I had ever done in all my life. I went through the most difficult struggles I have ever encountered in my entire life. For three-and-a-half years, which seemed like eternity, I was hardly even able to pray. During that very difficult time, I spent a lot of time looking towards the Lord, but not much time talking to Him. I went through a period of soul-searching that took me into a lot of areas in my life I had never experienced before. I was questioning my salvation and my sanctification. I was beginning to doubt, not only in myself and everything I was doing, but I was also doubting God. One day, about two years later, I was crying out to God. I came to the end of myself. I asked the Lord, "What am I going to do?" It seemed like all my dreams, all my hopes, and all my wishes had vanished. I had absolutely nothing to look forward to, except trying to survive.

During this time of total isolation from everything and everybody, I worked every day in a job requiring physical labour and hardships, which I had not done in twenty-five years. I would be so tired at the end of the day that I could hardly get out of my car and walk to the house. One of those days, the Lord spoke to me. He said, I want you to study about the twelve sons of Jacob." I knew this was God, because it was the last place my mind would have gone. I responded by saying to Him, "Why would I want to learn about a bad bunch of reprobates?" The Lord said to me, "Look at Revelation 21:10-27." The thing that stuck out to me was how those twelve men, at the end of their days, are referred to in Scripture as pearls. Pearls to me, were always very special jewels. I bought them for my wife. The reason I was partial towards the pearl is because I believed it was a living stone. The fact that these men, after what they had done with their lives and the way they had treated their Heavenly Father, could be referred to as pearls at the end of time, was totally fascinating to me.

So I began my study of what I called "The Twelve Sons of Jacob." I soon became totally involved, completely wrapped up in what I was learning. At first, I thought I was the only person who would ever involve themselves with the study of the twelve sons of Jacob. As I began to research what was out there in the book world, I found there was endless information and revelation floating around concerning the family of Jacob. Nevertheless, because God had told me to study about the twelve sons, I could not lay it down. As I read, it seemed like I was hearing these things for the first time. It was like a river of revelation was rolling into my mind every day. I was over-whelmed by the truth I was learning, because I thought I had learned all those things after fourteen years in the ministry. I was like a little boy in a candy shop or maybe a toy factory. I didn't know what to touch next; so I began to relate what I was learning, to my experience over the last fifteen years. I realized, after about three years, that a whole brand-new world of ministry had just opened up to me. It was a new lease on life; perhaps I was not ready to be buried yet. So, once again, I went back to my study time in the Word, and prayer, and seeking the Lord for the next four years. I had thought my world had ended, and now I was beginning to realize it actually, was only beginning.

By now, I had typed out about 2000 pages of research information concerning the twelve sons of Jacob. For sure the Lord wanted me to write a book about what I had dis-covered. My problem was that, whenever I sat down to write some of the things the Lord was showing me, I found it had already been published. After many years of soul-searching and asking the Lord what the point of all that work and time spent learning about something He had already revealed to someone else was, I began to feel I would never return to the ministry again. So, I put all the information in a box and set it behind my chair in my office, and thought that would be it. I gave a few copies of this information to some of my very close friends. They read it and offered me their honest opinion. They were very honest, but it was still very hard to accept.

Therefore, I set out on a quest. What was the point of researching and learning all this information? Life was passing me by. There were many interesting things I was doing. I was building golf courses all over the country, meeting a lot of very interesting people and, I might add, enjoying it for the most part, because during my period in the ministry, our family had gone into debt by about $40,000.00. Being back in secular work, I was able to start paying back some of these many bills and getting back on top financially. The Lord had given me a position and a paycheque whereby we were able to pay our bills, make a down-payment on a house, and move back into society again. It appeared at that time, that this would be the way I would devote my life.

Like most people, when things in your life change as drastically as mine did, you begin to do some reflecting. I had left a secular life of fifteen years and now I was back into it again. What happened during those fifteen years? After getting saved in 1979, our whole family came to the Lord. Within two months, I had gotten involved in the church to the point where I was involved in ministry. I became ordained; we went to Nova Scotia and planted a church, which was one of the best experiences our family ever had. We saw life in a way we had never experienced or even dreamed about. We saw things that were almost incomprehensible. My children finished their high school education and went to university. My oldest daughter got married and then, I burned out.

During the time of ministry, we had been given very little information on how to start a church, organize it, and manage it, to say the least. As frustrating as it was, we had nowhere to go but to the Lord. We came to the point where we prayed, asking the Lord about everything we should do, that we needed to do, and that He wanted us to do. I can truly say it was our way of life. "What would you have us do, Lord?" So now, I have come to the place where I believe I can share with people why the Lord led me in the study of the twelve sons of Jacob. God will never give up on anybody. Look at what the Lord has done and think about this: He will complete the good work that He has started in you. We would consider this at the beginning of every day.

On one occasion, I was flying from Toronto to Halifax. About an hour into the flight, I could hear a baby crying. Something was hurting him; it was a painful cry. It annoyed me so much, that I got up from my seat to see what was going on with this baby. I went to the back of the plane and then to the front, but there was no baby. But I could still hear it crying. About halfway back to my seat, I noticed a young woman sitting by herself and she was sobbing. The seat alongside her was empty, so I asked if I could sit by her, to which she agreed. I could still hear the baby crying. Trying to ignore it, I said to the young lady, "You seem to be very sad. I am a pastor. Maybe there is something I could pray about that might help you." She told me she was on her way to Halifax to have an abortion. She was pregnant and her boyfriend told her he would not marry her unless she aborted this baby. So she was going to have the abortion. I was able, by the grace of God, to convince her not to go through with this plan; that she should have the baby regardless of her boyfriend's request. To which she agreed.

At this point in time, the crying I was hearing ceased. No more crying baby. To make a long story short, about three weeks later, we were in church in Toronto when this young lady came in. She was very pregnant and told me she had decided to have the baby. This whole event in my life was totally transformational. I was almost afraid to tell people about this, for fear of what they would think of me, but I did share when it seemed appropriate.

On another occasion, one Sunday afternoon, I was having a rest when the phone rang and Denise, my wife, answered it. She woke me up and said a young man wanted to talk to me. He was a truck driver on his way from Fredericton, NB to Halifax, and he began to tell me about a very bad incident that had happened the night before between him and his wife and family. We spent about a half hour on the phone. I tried to comfort him. I could tell he was driving the truck. He asked me at that time if we had service on Sunday night. I told him that we did and where we were located. He said, "I'll probably see you tonight."

We went to church that night expecting this young man to show up, and he did. At the end of the service, I made an appeal for anyone who wanted to come to the altar for prayer, and he came forward. He had told me his, his wife's, and his children's names on the phone that afternoon. When he came forward for prayer, I said to him, "Have you been talking to your wife?" I named her and their children. He looked at me very surprised and said, "I don't know what you mean." I said, "You talked to me about your wife." Again I named her and his children. He said, "I'm sorry, why are you asking me this question?"

At this point, I became a little apprehensive. I reminded him of our phone call that afternoon when we had talked for more than half an hour about last night's situation and the problems that had been created with his wife and children. He insisted to me and my wife that he had not phoned anybody or told anybody about what I had just related to him. I apologized for being so forward.

He said to me, "What you are saying is all true, but I do not know how you know this, because we did not stop anywhere this afternoon coming from Fredericton to Halifax. We did not make a phone call to anyone." I believed his words. The Lord must have called me. I could not have possibly known this any other way.

It was then that we realized something supernatural was taking place. This young man rededicated his life to the Lord. We had a wonderful time of prayer and thanking God for His intervention. My last report from this man is that he was on his way to Bible school, had reunited with his family, and was committed to giving his life to the Lord's work.

One of the things I would like to mention here is that I had no former knowledge or information concerning this man and his situation. How then do I explain what happened on that particular Sunday afternoon? When I pray, I always ask my heavenly Father if there is something He would like to talk to me about and have me involved in. Sometimes I feel this prayer may be a ritual, and sometimes maybe not totally serious, but I pray it anyway, believing there may be someone crying out to God who needs an answer from Him. It is my conviction that God would like to use the Church to answer those prayers for help. So, I remain committed to praying my prayer and, staying close to the Lord, telling Him that should there be an occasion where He needs me, I would be available. And I leave it there. I do not go chasing through my idea library for things to do. I leave it with the Lord. This has happened many times to me—a simple phone call, a simple conversation. Without stress and anxiety, these things just happen and when they do it is an expression of the

Kingdom of God at work. My dear friend (reader) stay close to God in prayer. You never know when He may tap you on the shoulder for another divine encounter.

I am just going to give you one more story and, then, I want to explain what the Lord has shown me through all of this. A pastor friend of mine had invited me to come with them to Guatemala on a mission trip. He insisted it would be a great experience for me, which it really was. What I want to tell you about is not so much the trip itself, but what happened to me in order to go there. I had no money. He had already purchased the ticket, but I felt I could not go away for ten days to a place like that without any money. So I said to my wife, Denise, "Could you go visiting somewhere today, as I want to stay home in my office and talk to the Lord about this trip?" So she went out for the day and I went to my office to pray.

It was a long day and not much happened. I didn't get a word from the Lord. I really didn't get anything. My wife returned around 4:00 p.m. I heard her voice at the door and she asked me, "Where have you been today?" I said, "Right here in my office all day. Why do you ask? You had the car." She said, "I just met a man in the driveway and he gave me this envelope for you. He said he had been here twice before today, knocked on the door, and no one was home. 'So,' he said, 'I am glad you are here,' and gave me this envelope." I took the envelope from my wife. I opened it up quickly and there was $500.00—five $100 bills. I could not believe it. I ran to the door quickly to see if he was still there. There was no one in sight. I asked Denise who it was. She said, "I have no idea. I never saw him before." I looked at those five $100 bills. They had never been touched before. We could hardly believe what had just transpired. Interestingly, I went to Guatemala for ten days with my pastor friend, came back home, and still had the $500. We put it in the offering plate on Sunday and gave it back to the Lord.

We saw many people come to the Lord and grow in God's grace, to move on into ministry; and, now, it had all come to an end for me as I had said earlier. This was a time of reflection. During that time I studied about the twelve sons of Jacob, combined with the many supernatural events that had taken place. The Lord really wanted to show me something very important. There are so many things I feel I would like to share, but you would never get to the end of the book. I believe the Lord has given me an understanding of what is happening in the world around us, and what we need to do to prepare ourselves and the people of God for what is taking place. As I look at the events that took place, I think of the tribe of Issachar. The Bible tells us he knew what was wrong and he knew how to fix it. His name means "hired," or "he cannot be bought." When people are not for sale their integrity is always intact.

As I read over my notes on the twelve sons of Jacob and all the articles written by some great men and women of God, sharing the insights they received from the Lord, it seemed to me it would be time-consuming to write down here, in this book, all the things God has already told many other people. So with your permission, and I hope you read on, I want to share with you these things straight from my heart.

As I mentioned in my introduction, the Church, as we know it, is over. We have heard it preached, for many years, that God is doing a new thing. People are tired of hearing this, but let me assure you, God is in no hurry to please me or you with His agenda. God has a time, a place, a season, and people He will use to manifest His Kingdom to those that love them here on earth.

The time is now. Wherever you are is the place and the season of His appearing upon us.

CHAPTER 5

The Dawning of a New Day

When I began to study about Jacob and his twelve sons, I found it very, very, difficult to understand how in the world this family could possibly be the family of God. And thinking about the world we live in today—the culture and our society—how could you possibly think of Jacob's family? Think about the dysfunction. This man worked seven years for Rachel, then on his wedding night was deceived by Laban who sent Leah into him and he married the wrong woman. He decided to work for another seven years to get the woman he loved. In the meantime, he had six children by the woman he first married. He had four children by his concubines, and two more children by the woman he loves.

In my world, I do not believe I could describe anything more dysfunctional than this family. Yet God called them His children. I noticed that when each one of these children was born, they were given a name which was very meaningful. I am sure, at the time, it probably just seemed very natural—you have a child, you give it a name, and you move on to the next one, and so on; but this was a very special family and these are very special names. It is absolutely mind-blowing when you do an in-depth study of this family and its meaning even up to the world that we live in today. Many books have been written about this family and so, without repeating all that has been said, I want to share what the Lord showed me. I am putting this all out there for your scrutiny and yes, I'm going to allow you to judge it, and it is something here that applies to you considering your responsibility to God and what He might be saying to you.

It is my absolute belief that these twelve sons represent twelve revelations that God has revealed to His people to bring the Church to a Body of believers, unified in the Spirit of God, to do His will, to manifest His Kingdom here on earth, and to become the Bride of Christ, to whom Jesus will come one day and take home to Himself. I am just going to run through these twelve sons briefly.

Reuben is the firstborn, Simeon the second, Levi the third, Judah the fourth, Zebulun the fifth, Issachar the sixth, Dan the seventh, Gad the eighth, Asher the ninth, Naphtali the tenth, Joseph the eleventh, and Benjamin the twelfth and last son. In using the law of first mention, I would like to express their real meaning.

One of the first things I noticed is that each one of these boy's names is the name of a revelation. Reuben, who is the firstborn means "to be born again;" Simeon means "to be able to hear" or "to be Spirit-filled;" Levi's name means "joining" or "body ministry;" Judah means "to praise, to worship God." Zebulun's name means "habitation" or "dwelling place;" Issachar means "hired" or "reward;"

Dan means "to judge" or "to rule;" Gad means "a troop" or "good fortune;" Asher means "to be happy;" Naphtali means "to wrestle" or "to struggle;" Joseph means "he will add;" and Benjamin means "son of the right hand."

During revivals of the past, when a group of people received a revelation from the Lord, that revelation became very impactful and powerful in their lives. They built denominations around that revelation, and this is how our denominations were formed. Hear me out. Some churches believe only in salvation (Reuben)—you only need to get saved and wait for your graduation to heaven. Is it any wonder there is difficulty in those places? The Bible says Reuben, on his own, was as unstable as water. If all you have experienced as a Christian is salvation, yes, you will go to heaven when you die, but you will not have a full Christian life. Other churches believe in salvation and a Pentecostal experience and have built a denomination around that. Other churches have added body ministry to this dimension. Other churches have added Judah to this, which is praise and worship music singing, and building a denomination around that, and so on. Some people have taken a revelation, built a denomination around it, sealed the door, and built the box.

Revelation 21, says the City of God has twelve entrances, twelve revelations, twelve experiences, and twelve gates—however you want to spell it out; but in order to enter into the Holy City of God, you need to open your heart to all twelve revelations. I believe that, when Jesus said He would build His Church and the gates of hell would not prevail against it, this is what He was referring to. The description in the Book of Revelation is very clear. It is a holy place, a place where God dwells; it is a place where God administers His Kingdom for a place that should be very visible to Christian believers, with attributes and virtues that are only there, and no place else.

As we continue our study of the Book of Revelation and what goes on in the Kingdom of God, I find it very, very difficult to understand why some churches resist Pentecost. Pentecost is not a denomination and neither should any of the other revelations be a denomination. Pentecost is the means by which God speaks to His Church by His Spirit. God will do nothing in the earth today concerning His Kingdom without the Holy Spirit. Jesus said: "I'm going back to the Father, and when I get there He will send the Holy Spirit to you. He will lead and guide you, and teach you all things about the Kingdom of God, and He will use Me (Jesus) to describe that to you; if you do not believe in the manifestation of the Holy Spirit through the nine gifts He possesses, how in the world do you expect to demonstrate the Kingdom of God?"

It would appear to me that the denominations who call themselves churches, get along with each other today much the same as Jacob's twelve sons got along with each other. It is a pretty sorry tale when you read the history of the children of Israel—how God blessed them, and how they turned their backs on Him. Yet, He continued to bless them. It is hard to believe and to think that there could be so much grace and mercy available to mankind when we believe in the Lord Jesus Christ.

I said at the beginning, "It's all about Jesus." It was God's plan, after the fall of Adam, to send His Son, Jesus, into the world to redeem mankind back to Himself. I don't believe that anybody could possibly fully comprehend all the dynamics involved in this process; therefore, I believe God made it simple and gave us four chapters—Matthew, Mark, Luke, and John—which give us a description of His Son, the Lord Jesus. He gives us the challenge that, if we would believe on the Lord Jesus Christ and confess Him with our mouth, we would be saved. This means that we would have eternal life and that life could be lived in the presence of God, under the tutelage of the Holy Spirit, managed by God Himself.

An interesting thing took place. This nation of Israel that had the blessing of God on them, came to a place that, when the famine came, they didn't trust God. If you are a believer, you know what happened when they went to Egypt, and how God delivered them from Egypt and brought them back to Canaan through the wilderness. The history of it all is extraordinary. But the Lord showed me here that, when the time of famine came, it was not because they had no money; it was because they were lazy and had disobeyed God. God used the famine to pull His people back together as a family, and to show them He still loved them; He cared for them, and He still wanted them to be the example of heaven here on earth to all the other nations in the world.

As we read in Ephesians, God's will is that the Church (twelve revelations, twelve experiences, twelve sons) would come together and be one Church under God, obeying Him and manifesting His presence. God has given the Church everything it needs for this to take place. But as long as the Church, as we know it today, continues to segregate itself in its individual ways, not having anything to do with each other—whether through a secular means or a spiritual means—they cannot fulfill the purpose and plan God has for the people on earth today. This is the reason I believe it is so important for believers to put God first in everything they do, and allow the Holy Spirit to become so real in their lives that they will be able to communicate to Him and through Him, just as people did with Jesus when He was here on earth.

Jesus said this: "When the Holy Spirit has come, the Holy Spirit can lead and guide you in all things, and everything you have seen Me (Jesus) do, you will be able to do, because He (the Holy Spirit) will be with you; and greater things than I have done, you will do." So many churches believe this is only possible when we get to heaven. Jesus taught us, through the Disciples' Prayer, how to pray so that we can have heaven's benefits while we live here on earth. If this was not the case then why would He teach us to pray this way? Consider this, "Thy Kingdom come, Thy will be done on earth as it is in heaven." This raises a question—Why would God tell us to pray like that if it were not possible to experience heaven's Kingdom on earth? Why would He raise our expectations during the here and now if we are only supposed to receive our answer after we die and get to heaven? The churches that teach that the Kingdom of God is being revealed here on earth, are churches or groups of believers who are truly in touch with God.

I would like to take a moment right here and say to you who are reading this book—by now you will have noticed that I have not included all the Scripture references for you to see. My reason for this is very deliberate. The Kingdom of God is more than one verse or even a combination of a few verses. The Kingdom of God is bigger than twelve men who were born to a man in Israel a long time ago, whose names speak of revelations from God. Yet, I would see in Scripture things like, "Fear not little flock for it is the Lord's good pleasure to give to you the Kingdom." What an awesome statement! You should look that up and the context of what it really means.

Yes, this book I'm trying to write is a story from my experience, and it's all about Jesus. He is the author and finisher of our whole life and the story we are part of, praise God. God supplied the manna and all the things the children of Israel needed. They did not know how to fend for themselves. There are many Christians today who do not know how to get the gold from Golgotha. We are so blessed with so many wonderful Bible teachers who paid the price of searching the Scriptures and gave us the gold. It seems we can just buy a book and we have it all.

I believe we have come to a period of time where God wants us to go into each word—not just read it, but talk to Him about what you are reading, and allow Him to invade your very presence with revelation knowledge, so that you can truly declare "we have the mind of Christ;" therefore, when these events begin to take place, you will be no stranger when God taps you on the shoulder and says, "Come, we have work to do."

Yes, I do believe that the Kingdom of God can be revealed to the Church for the people in the world right now. The best way I know how to do this is to tell them about Jesus Christ—who He is and who He was when here on earth; what He did while He was here, the commands He left us to fulfill; and that we should do these things, and have them done when He comes to get us. I mentioned three stories or events that took place in my life concerning the Kingdom of God. I could list twenty-five similar events, and I do not believe that would be all. This should be the normal life of a Christian believer in the Church of the Lord Jesus Christ.

Many people look at the Church today and tell me it is irrelevant and, for the most part, I almost have to agree with them. Most churches today have occupied and are occupying their time as a slave to their denomination, trying to maintain that one truth and that one revelation they received. Is it everything we need? I asked the questions: "Is there a famine of the Spirit in the Church today? Are you familiar with the moving of the Spirit of God? Are you seeing blind people healed, deaf people hearing, dumb people talking, lame people walking, sick people being healed, demon-possessed people being delivered, and people being raised from the dead? Are you seeing people being saved from their sin, delivered from the power of sin and the fear of hell? Are you seeing these things take place in your church?" If not, then I ask you, how can you pray and say, "Thy will be done, oh Lord, on earth even as it is in heaven?" If the church group you are going to and worshipping with does not **believe** these things, I believe you are part of the harlot Church. It has a form of godliness but it denies the power of God. You are ever learning, but never coming to the knowledge of who Christ really is, and what the Church is really all about. You are part of that group that Paul speaks about when he says, "If you partake of the Lord's table in an unworthy manner, you are asleep and maybe even dead to the things of God."

I think it is a wonderful thing to be able to give clothes and food to those people who really do not have any, and to help them in any way; and, it is possible, even the world does that. But it is the Church's responsibility to do things that lead people to eternal life and faith in Jesus Christ, because, without that, you can gain the whole world and lose your soul. Although things may seem so disjointed, and so dysfunctional, the time has come when people in the Church are going to come together with one message and one purpose, serving one God, one Lord, and one Saviour, Jesus Christ; and when this begins to happen, God will add all the other things we need.

CHAPTER 6

In the Presence of God

One of the most important things that we Christians can do is to pray. To pray simply means to communicate to our Heavenly Father the things that are concerning us and, in the process of doing this, we could ask the Father to share the things that concern Him. During this process we should be inquiring of the Lord what He is telling us we could do concerning His interest. Far too often, we really never ask the Father what He is thinking about concerning us and our situation; we do a lot of uploading and leaving it with the Lord. One day as I was praying, I was asking the Lord to do many things; I paused, and heard the Lord say to me, "Some of those things that you have asked Me to do, I have already asked you to do."

One day the disciples came to Jesus and said to Him, "Master, teach us to pray like you do." I have often wondered why they asked this question, but through studying the Word I could see what the difference was. Jesus was getting answers from the Father to do things and they were not. This concerned them to the point that they wanted to get answers like Jesus did, so they asked Him to teach them to pray like He prayed. "Our Father which art in heaven, hallowed be thy name. Thy Kingdom come, thy will be done, as in heaven, so in earth. Give us this day our daily bread. And forgive us our sins; we also forgive everyone that is indebted to us. And lead us not into temptation; but deliver us from evil." Now over in Matthew 6:13 this prayer is finished with these words. *For thine is the kingdom, and the power and the glory, forever amen.*

This has become to me one of the greatest things I have ever discovered in God's Word.

Being able to sit down and discuss daily issues with the Creator of the universe, is almost impossible to believe. But unless you do this, you will never know, and never understand the tremendous freedom that will be released in your life and in your circumstances. One of the greatest books I have read on this prayer was written by Larry Lea called, *Could you not Tarry One Hour?* I believe that every Christian should have this book and study it. I spent a lot of time thanking the Lord for what He gave Larry Lea on this issue of prayer and how he was able to show us how important it is for believers to take this truth to heart.

I am trying to relay to you how important and useful this book is to me, still today. It has helped me to find my way into the presence of God in such a way that I know He is with me. There is such a large discussion today over feelings, and our senses. Is there a difference? Yes there is, and I would just like to say that there is nothing quite like sensing the presence of God. As one dear old preacher said one time, "It is better felt then telt." One of the many things I learned through prayer is that the more you do it the better and more meaningful your relationship with the Lord becomes. One day as I was praying, the Lord spoke to me. He said, "I will teach you how to handle My presence." It was at that moment I realized, that if I knew how to act in the presence of the Lord, I could handle any situation that came my way. What a tremendous relief that was because, at that time, I had a habit of placing some people I knew in a category of social standing they did not deserve, and I did not know how to handle it. So I began to pray and ask the Lord to show me through His Word about His presence and how I should respond—how to live and abide in His presence. This has changed my entire relationship with the Lord and my entire outlook on life.

For the rest of this chapter I want to indulge you in some of the things the Lord is showing me. The reason for this is that I believe, now, more than ever before, we have to be so sensitive to the presence of God and the function of the Holy Spirit in our lives so that we can truly say as our Lord would say, "I only did the things My Father told me, and whatever He told Me to do I did."

I began to understand when Moses asked the Lord, "Would you go with us as we journey from Egypt to Canaan," and the Lord said His presence would go with them all the time. Moses responded to this promise, saying, "If Your presence does not go with us, we might as well stay here." Those are my words, but this is the truth; if we are not living in the presence of God, we are outside of the will of God.

Exodus 33:14 *"My presence will go with you"* (NKJV). Leviticus 26:12 tells us, *"And I will walk among you, and will be your God, and you shall be my people [in this pilgrimage of life]"* (NKJV). God gives us the courage we need, knowing that the Lord is with us. He will protect us and He will keep us throughout our journey. He will never leave us nor forsake us. What I learned here about the presence of God is that there is always an awareness of His presence, through an inward grasp of the Holy Spirit, through an inward working of faith in my heart, and to an inward birthing of the things of the Spirit. God reveals His secrets to His friends; He releases revelation of His desires and what He wills us to do.

Fellowship with God is governed by the light we received. No longer are we walking in darkness, because the light has come, and we now have fellowship with the Father. In fellowship with the Father and with His Son, Jesus Christ, we therefore, abide in light (with understanding); we walk in the light, we move in light and, when we want to know more and more of the person and the nature of the things that are eternal, we must then spend more time in prayer with Him. Humanity will stagger at the revelation of the wonders of God's wisdom in the midst of His Church. Truly God's plan is great! The outcome is going to be even greater than anything we have ever heard or understood. Yes, there will be sacrifice, and there will be great effort put forward, so that we may comprehend that for which we have been apprehended. We begin to realize that we are privileged to walk with God, to sing praises to Him, demonstrate the gladness of our hearts, and show appreciation for salvation that He has so freely given us. What an amazing thought, that Jesus loves me.

It is good to remind ourselves, as often as we can, that God has called us to a high and holy calling—called to be saints, children of God, set apart, separated from the world, able to demonstrate in our lives the highest standard of life available to mankind. All because of the abiding presence of God with us. One of the most astounding thoughts is that God is not just with us, but He is in us; fellowship with God is the secret of Christian living. To have Christ indwelling you in His power, love, and grace has to be the greatest confidence builder any human can have. In 1 John 4:12 the Bible tells us that God dwells in us. 1 Corinthians 3:16 tells us, *"Know you not that you are the temple of God and that the Spirit of God lives in you?"* We can have victory over every situation in life because God is with us; triumph and not tragedy should be the experience of every child of God.

Every Christian needs a fresh vision of the Lord Jesus Christ to awaken them to the unsearchable riches in Christ. Jesus has so much to show us and to make known to us, as we spend time with Him in prayer, recognizing He is the Lord. He will show us the treasures of the glorious Godhead and how we are to make the Lord known to the world we live in. Paul reminds us in 1 Corinthians 2:9, *"Eye hath not seen, nor ear heard, neither have entered into the heart of man, the things which God hath prepared for them that love him."* There is no higher life and no greater fellowship for mankind beyond the known presence of God. Enoch walked with God, and one day, he just walked into heaven; Noah was a just man in his generation, the Bible says. Noah walked with God. We can also walk with God. We can walk in the new life, we can walk in faith, we can walk honestly, we can walk with the knowledge of God, and we can honour God's commandments knowing that there is a life after death that is beyond comprehension to the human mind. Can we realize the privilege that is ours so that we can enjoy it? Imagine walking daily in fellowship with our Creator. How awesome it is to be called the friend of God, companion of God, someone you can talk to about absolutely everything you could imagine and think about. We have fellowship with God through our conversations in prayer. In Malachi 3:16 we read that *"they that feared the Lord spake often one to another: and the Lord hearkened [to what they were saying and their names were recorded in his book of remembrance]."* We have fellowship with God in the secret place—that means I can talk to Him directly about things in my life that I would be absolutely afraid to talk to anybody else about, knowing that He would hear me, and answer me, and not condemn me. That is what being a friend of God really means.

We receive protection from those things that might harm us. Many are the afflictions of the people of God but the Lord will deliver us from all of them. He will give us courage to stand firm in the midst of any persecution as we walk with God. His divine presence will give us the strength we need, and the will we must have, so that we can address the situations we are facing with the Word of God that we learn as we study. We will be able to use His Word to defend ourselves and to ward off any enemies such as: doubt, unbelief, fear, any old pressure of the enemy. We can use His Word and be set free.

There are so many things I have learned about the presence of God. These are evil days we are living in. The enemy is roaming up and down the earth, seeking whom he may devour and saying many things that are not true. It appears he has the freedom to do whatever he likes; but, my friends, I have discovered that in the presence of God, the devil cannot steal your joy or take away your peace, because in God's presence is fullness of joy and at His right hand are pleasures forevermore. We can expect to learn new things, have new experiences, and see new things concerning the Kingdom of God every day. The Bible says He will go before us, He will lead us Himself. He does not send us on our own, but He leads us. When we make a mistake, we can be like David and say, "Cast me not away from Your presence, O Lord, and take not Your Holy Spirit from me." Therefore come into His presence with thanksgiving and make a joyful noise unto the Lord. Serve the Lord with gladness as you come into His presence, singing.

I have come to understand, through the study of God's Word, that I am going to live forever when I leave this earth. I am going to spend eternity with my God in heaven. This is awesome. Yes, prayer is simple. It is quietly opening a door and slipping into a room with God. He is sitting in the middle of the room waiting for you to enter. And there, in the stillness of that room, you will hear that small voice that would say to you, "Welcome. I have been waiting for you."

I began to wonder, concerning the presence of God, how I should behave, what I should say, what I could take away from this meeting? People in the New Testament said that when they met the Christians, they knew that they (Christians) had been with Jesus. This is what I want to take away from every time I pray—that people will know I have spent time with Jesus. The Lord has shown me in the Scriptures that if I will obey the voice of God, no human being will ever be able to withstand or confront me, for God will take part. So many times in Scripture we see where God's people were so overwhelmed and out-numbered by the opposition, but when they took time to seek the Lord, though they were few in number, the Lord gave them the victory. We have that same promise today. We face many Goliaths, we face many enemies in life, but God will deliver us from them all.

Practicing the presence of God in your life every day, I believe, is the formula for a successful Christian life. This is the only way to walk pleasing to God. God's smile will be upon you, you will be fruitful in every good work, you will increase in the knowledge of God, you will find patience, long-suffering, joyfulness to be desired; you will become spiritually strong in the power of His might; you will be able to find forgiveness much easier; you will be able to find repentance more necessary and much easier; you will find fellowshipping with the saints a necessity; you will be so blessed whenever you read the Word and hear people talking about the Lord Jesus; your attitude will be to please God rather than men; you will grow in the knowledge of our Lord and Saviour, and He will give you the wisdom you need to deal with this knowledge.

Knowledge without wisdom can be deadly. We need the presence of God with us at all times.

These are just a few of the blessings that are ours. Paul said, "I am not ashamed of the gospel of Jesus Christ, for it is the power of God unto salvation to the Jew first and then to the Gentiles." My question is, "Do you know this? Are you aware of how this is manifested in your life?" This has been one of my greatest experiences. I realize that many people are praying about certain things that are very concerning to them and to people that are around them; it could be for a sickness, a financial issue, or a relational problem. Many people are praying about many, many things, and it is my absolute conviction that God wants to answer their prayers. His number one way of doing this is through His Church. God wants the world to be able to look at the Church and recognize Jesus.

Remember the Church that was founded in Antioch? Scripture tells us, the people of Antioch called them Christians because they acted like Jesus. It is my conviction that if the Church is doing its job, it will be recognized as people who have spent time with Jesus. God needs to be able to speak to somebody in the Church, who He has gifted with some special grace, to go and meet the needs of those praying for His help, so their prayer can get answered. I know there are many ways, and God is not limited in answering our prayers, but what a tremendous thrill to be that person. Then, one day in their life, God would be able to speak into their ear and say, "I need you to go there. They have been asking me for help. I need you to go there and take a message to them."

One day I was sitting in the house having a cup of tea with my wife when I felt the Lord say to me, "You should go visit this friend of yours." It did not seem like a big deal, but I knew it was the Lord prompting me, so Denise agreed. She said it would be a good idea. So off I went, and as I was going, the Lord spoke to me and gave me a Scripture. He said, "When you get there read this Scripture to your friend." I thought, "Wow! This is awesome! Yes, Lord, I will do this."

Upon arriving at his house, I knocked on the door. I could hear shouting and a loud proclamation from within the house. I thought maybe I should leave and come back another day, but I felt the Lord saying, "Knock again." So

I knocked again and the shouting stopped. It was quiet and then I saw the door open. My friend stood in the doorway looking at me with a tear-drenched face, exhausted, and very pale. I told him that perhaps I should come at another time. He could hardly talk but he managed to say, "Please, please come in and have a seat."

When I got in the house I realized he was all alone so I wondered who he was talking to. Curiosity got the best of me, so I asked my friend, "Who were you talking to before I came in?" He said, "I was talking to the Lord. I have been talking to Him all night and all day. Why have you come here?" I told him, "I was sitting at home and the thought came to me that I should come visit you. Denise agreed and here I am." I continued, "I don't know what's going on but I believe that God has sent me, because on the way here He gave me a Scripture, and told me to read it to you when I got here." It was Jeremiah 29:11-13. At that point, he broke down, fell on the floor, and began to weep and weep, at times uncontrollably. I began to call out to the Lord for wisdom and understanding as to how I could help my friend. "You have sent me, Lord. Tell me what to do."

After a while, he calmed down and showed me in his open Bible, which was laying on the table, that the Lord had just given him that verse ten minutes before I arrived. In the midst of all our despair, at that moment, we rejoiced. He kept saying over and over, "The Lord heard me. The Lord heard me." He continued saying this over and over, and all I could do was sit there and wonder what was going on. This poor man was so broken, and now he is so happy; what had changed?

We continued to talk and he shared his dilemma with me. God was able to give me some words of wisdom and encouragement that would bring him hope and restore unto him the joy of the Lord. This poor man was facing a difficult situation and he did not know if he could continue any longer this way. But now, his hope had been restored, only because it was confirmed to him that the Lord heard his cry; the Lord had answered him on what to do, and how to resolve the situation. He was so happy that the Lord heard him. He declared to me, this was the first time in his life he really believed that God heard and answered prayer. We had a great time of fellowship. I am not sure what his status is today. That is not my responsibility. My responsibility was to hear God speak to me that day and go to my friend.

Dear friends, I could share many stories like that with you—different people, yet similar situations; of how God sent me to them and when I got there, the Lord was waiting for me. This is why I believe prayer is so essential and necessary today for the Church, so that we can become so sensitive to God's presence that we can probably feel His breath, hear His voice, and be able to respond with confidence that He has spoken. We must be certain that this is the Word of the Lord. This only happens by spending time alone with God in prayer, allowing His presence to overcome you, and being able to sense at the slightest that God is present. Pay attention, and remember that God knows everything before it happens. He knows what is going to happen, and He knows how it continues. Are you one of those the Lord can tap on the shoulder at any time and say, "Let's go, we have work to do?" This, to me, is what I have learned about the presence of God. What a confidence builder and a strength it is. For the eye has not seen nor ear heard, neither has it yet entered into the heart of man the things that God has yet to reveal to the Church.

Yes, by practicing the presence of God, you will be able to serve the Lord with gladness; you will experience joy that is unspeakable and full of glory; you will know what it is to have abundant life; your heart will throb at the thrill of the Holy Spirit quickening your mortal body, witnessing to you in your spirit that you are a child of God. The unsaved will see and know that there is a God in heaven. The saints will be blessed in their time of trouble, the Church will be edified and built up in the most holy faith, and the Church will progress from glory to glory in God's eternal purpose, which He has purposed in the Church through Christ Jesus. The saints will begin to understand the mystery of God's will, and they will begin to receive revelation, knowledge, and supernatural wisdom. The eyes of their understanding will become enlightened as they see the riches of God's Kingdom manifested through them. As I said earlier, it is important that we understand what it is to walk with God. To walk before God is a walk of duty. To walk after God, is the walk of discipleship. To walk with God is a walk of devotion. We walk by faith not by sight; we walk in the Spirit, not in the flesh. When we become consistent in our faith, it is a walk of love; it is a walk of extended light; it is a walk of truth.

By living in the presence of God, we can expect God's divine direction and we can experience God's faithfulness. In His presence, we will experience encouragement, know His protection over us and, in a loving way, we will see our invincibility. To love God is to obey God; and to worship God is to never argue with the will of God. The blessing of obedience brings absolute peace, not only with

God, but within ourselves and with all those around us. That is something that we, as Christians, can experience and others will enjoy. Looking back in the Scriptures to some of the people that God used, we see the following people: Enoch, who walked with God; David was a man after God's own heart; Joshua followed the Lord; Daniel was greatly beloved; Samuel was called by God, sent by God, listened to God, and laboured for God. It is so impressive how these men of God enjoyed the presence of the Lord. There was Ananias, a true disciple of the Lord, and Paul and Silas, who demonstrated praying and praising God under tremendous circumstances and seeing God answer. We, as the Church, can learn from the experiences of God's servants. The Lord God blessed them with the Holy Spirit and with His presence, and by what He was able to do through them and by them. He can do the same through the Church.

As we come to the New Testament, there are so many people we could talk about. We just mentioned Ananias. He was the guy God used to speak to Paul after he got saved. When Paul got saved, Paul didn't have a lot of friends, but God knew Ananias' heart. God knew that He could speak to Ananias, and he would talk to Paul. Ananias prayed for Paul and the scales fell off his eyes, and Paul received his sight.

In the New Testament and in our lives today, it is different than it was in Old Testament times (when God would anoint a special person to carry out a special mission on His behalf) because today, the Bible tells us that God pours out His Spirit upon all flesh. There is no discrimination. There is no separation. Peter stated this as he preached his first sermon. This is what was spoken of by the prophet Joel, "that in the last days God would pour out His Spirit upon all flesh, your sons and your daughters shall prophesy, your young men shall have visions and your old men shall dream dreams." This is the blessing God has given to His Church in these days. Some of the ways by which God speaks to His Church and through His Church are through visions and dreams. The time is coming when, more than ever, it will be important for the Church to function in this way. One of the things I have experienced in my walk with the Lord, is that you cannot become successful spiritually without the discipline of the Holy Spirit in your life. Only through such discipline and self-denial can a person come to this precious, precious experience of handling the presence of God.

I want to conclude this chapter with another little story. This happened one Sunday morning in our church as we were preparing to break bread. I was at the front of the church during the service, preparing the emblems and watching over the congregation as the elders were serving the Communion. I was praying that everybody who partook that morning would realize how important it was to themselves and to the Lord. Normally during the services, everything is fairly routine—you break the bread, you give a plate to each one of the elders, they serve everybody, and bring the plates back. We partake of the broken bread representing the body of Christ and, then, we serve the wine representing the shed blood of the Lord Jesus. Then, we pray a prayer of faith, thanksgiving, and blessing over the congregation.

On this particular Sunday morning, as I was praying, the Lord spoke to me that there was a young family in the church. They had just had a new baby and the baby had problems. Their baby was crying day and night for several weeks and they were exhausted. The Lord spoke to me and said, "Tell the father to go into the nursery and bring in the baby. I want to heal her." So, I stopped the Communion service at that point and instructed the father to go and bring his child. While he was going to the nursery to get the baby, I had a visit from the enemy who said to me, "What are you going to do now?" This was his accusation and question. I must admit I heard that. I asked the Lord, "What am I going to do now?" And the Lord said, "Ask the congregation if they have a prayer, a word, or a Psalm." It was like a wave came over the congregation and everybody spontaneously got up and quoted a Scripture and shared a thought or a Psalm. It just went around the room. It was beautiful. It was the presence of the Lord.

Then I told the father to bring the baby to me, up to the front. I took the baby in my arms and it stopped crying. It was beautiful. Then I asked the Lord, "What am I going to do now?" And the Lord said, "Give the baby back to the father. I have healed it." I followed His instructions. The father took the baby back to the nursery and the baby went to sleep. We continued with Communion and thanked the Lord for His presence at our meeting and for giving this family their peace. On Tuesday night of that week, they came to the service and gave a testimony of how the baby was sleeping, how God had healed it, and how wonderful life was so that they could enjoy their baby and each other again.

I am telling you this story because, when the Lord is teaching you how to handle His presence, He is going to ask you to do things that are not traditional and, perhaps, may break the rules. When the rules and your denominational doctrine are too important, you cannot make any changes and the Lord cannot break in and answer prayer. That is really what He wants to do. He wants to answer prayer and manifest His presence, to bring joy and peace to His family, the Church, the Body of Christ, the descendants of Jacob.

Jesus Christ shows us, in the Gospels, what a relationship with our heavenly Father can be like, and tells us that we can have the same relationship with our heavenly Father that He, Jesus Himself had. But when our rules and rituals, and the fear of man become more important than God's purposes in the Church, it is difficult for the Church to do its job as the Body of Christ. I pray that as you read this, you may hear the heart of God open up to you. Get used to handling the presence of God; invite Him into every situation you are involved with, whether at home, at work, or even at church. Allow the Holy Spirit to manifest the presence of God to you so that you may truly be a co-labourer with Christ in building His Church. Amen.

CHAPTER 7

The Throne Room of God

The Bible tells us that in the last days God will pour out His Spirit upon all flesh, our sons and daughters will prophesy, our young men shall see visions, and our old men shall dream dreams. God will show wonders in the heaven above, signs in the earth beneath, and whosoever shall call upon the name of the Lord will be saved. It is very difficult to grasp hold of the idea that God could possibly show me something that is going on in heaven that needs to take place on earth; yet, I believe that most of my ministry is somehow wrapped up in the Kingdom of God being revealed to mankind today.

One day, I was praying and talking to the Lord about the idea of judging. So many people today say it is not only wrong to judge, but, maybe, it is a sin. This drew me to much prayer and waiting upon the Lord. As I was praying, the Lord gave me a vision. It was one of the most vivid pictures I had ever looked at in my life. I was able to study it, while it was in my mind, to the point that I could describe it in minute detail. God was pointing something out to me that was unparalleled to anything I had heard or studied before. Here is the picture of what I saw: a friend of mine, who is a graphic artist, listened as I explained, and was able to put together this drawing as you see it on the page. This is as near perfect to what I saw as I could get it.

My first thoughts, when I began to examine this vision, were almost shocking. Whatever happened to the Ten Commandments? How is it possible for some teachers to say that we are no longer under the Law, but under grace? Throw the Law away; we are now in grace. I was reminded that our Saviour said, "I have not come to do away with the Law; I have come to fulfill it." In bringing to mankind a brand-new covenant, the old must first be fulfilled or completed. Therefore, in fulfilling the new covenant, the Law is complete. By fulfilling the most important Law of all, which was the first Law ever given—To love the Lord your God with all your heart, with all your soul, and with all your might—and, the second commandment—Thou shalt love thy neighbour as thyself. As I continued to study this vision the Lord had given me, I realized the most important word here is "truth."

Without truth everything else is completely redundant. Pilate asked our Lord, "What is truth?"

He was implying that perhaps there was no such thing; but Jesus said to him, "I am the truth."

John tells us in his Gospel that grace and truth both came by Jesus Christ. The Law was given by Moses, but truth and grace came with Jesus Christ. As we look at this picture, we see in the forefront the Ark of the Covenant, with the angels hovering over the mercy seat; inside the

Ark are the Ten Commandments, the manna that came down from heaven, and Aaron's rod that budded.

Scripture tells us that one day every knee will bow and every tongue will confess that Jesus Christ is Lord, to the glory of God the Father. Before you can stand before the judgment seat of Christ, you must pass by the Ark of the Covenant. The Ark of the Covenant represents the promises of God, the provision of God, and the power of God. Many great teachers have taught on these subjects. There are more books than you could possibly count on what I have just described to you. Can you imagine finding yourself, one day, standing all by yourself on that floor of justice, not knowing Jesus Christ as your Saviour?

Having heard the Gospel, and now facing the judgment of God, if you don't know Jesus Christ as your Saviour and Lord, take time right now; lay the book aside and introduce yourself to your Saviour and Redeemer, and make it right with God.

Consider this with me as you look at these judges. Don't ask me why there were twelve and why these were the ones shown. This is what I saw in the vision and I am going to talk to you about it. The Bible tells us clearly to judge yourself so that you don't need to be judged. To me that is frightening, because I do not know how to judge myself. However, when I looked at this vision, all of a sudden, I could judge myself. I have a benchmark. You have a benchmark—morals, dignity, trust, honour, hope, grace, integrity, courage, respect, ethics, gratitude, and justice (the fruit of the Law). If people think these things no longer matter, they are in for a big surprise. The Lord spoke to me saying, "This is the fruit of the Law." We have the fruit of the Spirit—love, joy, peace, long-suffering, gentleness, goodness, faith, meekness, and temperance; against such there is no law. For those judges to be satisfied, they will be looking for the fruit of the Spirit in the fruit of the Law. It is my strongest conviction that when I stand in front of those judges, every one of them will say to me, "Guilty;" but when I look up and see Jesus on the throne, I believe He will tell the judges, "He is mine. Bring him in. I paid for all of his sin and he is free to enter into heaven. Come and join with the heavenly hosts this day."

Maybe I have gotten off track. You think, "But how could any of this take place without a judge?" Before the Law was given, Scripture tells us, in Genesis 6, that God saw that the wickedness of man was great in the earth and that every imagination of the thoughts of his heart was only evil continually. There were no restraints. Man did whatever he liked. No disciplining actions took place. So the Lord sent the flood, and He started afresh with Noah and his family. Along came Abraham with Isaac and Jacob and here is where we will pick it up again.

As we consider the fruit of the Law, realize that this cannot be possible without God's grace and mercy operating, even back in those days. It would appear that grace and mercy were hidden because of the Law. Dan, who is now the seventh son of Jacob, seems to shed some light on the situation. Rachel said to Jacob, "Give me children or I'll die." She told him, "Behold my handmaid, Bilha. Go in unto her and she will bear upon my knees, so that I will also have children by her." And so, she gave her handmaid to Jacob as a wife. She conceived and bore a son. Rachel said, "God has judged me," and therefore named him "Dan," meaning "to be judged." When you do a search on this name, you find that it means "an empire to execute judgment." You also find the word, "Adonia." This word means "master or lord." Dan was called to be a judge with the lordship as a ruler. As we pass through this experience of Dan in our Christian life, we get to begin to appreciate what it means to judge. I appreciate how close Dan is to Issachar, who cannot be bought. In John 7:24 (NKJV) we read, *"Do not judge according to appearance, but judge with righteous judgement"* from that Christ-nature within you, and from there will come forth the pureness of the Law, which will produce the Law of Scripture. It will also contain the fruit of the Spirit, and the judgment will be righteous.

Matthew 7:3-5 says, "Why behold the mote that is in your brother's eye but consider not the beam that is in your own. Pull the mote out of your own eye, and then you can see clearly and honestly how to cast the mote out of your brother's eye." This chapter gives us great insight on the matter of judgment. This is very clear in making decisions in life. Discipline is never punishment; discipline is meant for protection, guidance, and assistance in living life—never judgment. Many Christians grow up today not knowing the difference between discipline and judgment; and may God, by His Holy Spirit, reveal this to all of us, so that we can walk in the discipline of God's Word and not be found under the judgment of sin. Moreover, Dan was one of the pearl gates into the City of God. Yes, we must pass this gate in order to enter into the City of God. This is a revelation that must become an experience in the heart of every believer, in order to truly appreciate the grace and mercy of God. We must pass through this gate. So let us inquire of the Lord and get His advice on how to proceed.

Our self-examination should take us to the pattern of the life of Christ—how He humbled Himself and became a man, and took upon Himself my sin. He died on the cross for me and was raised from the dead. My unrighteous judgment was laid on Him, so that I could be free from that judgment if I could believe in Him. This Dan nature from within me will say, "I'm going to wait upon the Lord." I will continue to wait until the wee small voice speaks from within, from God's throne to my heart and, then, I will give an answer. We have made so many wrong decisions because we failed to inquire of the Lord and wait.

Scripture tells us that God's judgments are unsearchable. This is why we need the Holy Spirit working within us constantly, in order to help us understand our situations that are so unsearchable by our human nature. Only God, by His Holy Spirit, can truly search our hearts and find God's way and, thereby, direct us in every situation we face in life. We have to be so careful, because we have a tendency to compare spiritual things with earthly things. Paul teaches us that the natural man receives not the things of the Spirit of God, for they are foolishness to him, and neither can he know them because they are only spiritually discerned by the servant's spiritual ability to judge all things.

In Genesis 49, the Word tells us Dan will judge His people. So what is God's purpose for Dan to the people of God? Today Dan has been given the ministry to judge the truth. It was said about Dan that he would be like a serpent by the way, he would bruise the heel of the ministry, but the ministry will crush the serpent's head. We need to be wise as serpents but harmless as doves. The ministry of

Dan is to separate sin from the sinner. When this ministry of this revelation stops, it becomes a denomination. It takes on wisdom of its own and perverts the truth for its own gain. This is that ministry that causes the riders on horseback to fall backwards, to be overwhelmed, broken, and bruised.

Saints of God, judgment begins in the house of God. That does not mean where you go to worship; that means in our own hearts. We have to have the experience to relate. We can also draw from the experience of ancient men and women who have gone before us. We also have the experience of the Lord Jesus Christ to help us, and we also have the Holy Spirit in these days to prevent a wonderful ministry from becoming perverted and useless. Here are some Scriptures that you might want to look up yourself and meditate over: Psalm 25:3-5, Psalm 27:14, Psalm 37:9, and 34, Psalm 39:1-9, Psalm 52:9, Psalm 69:6, and Psalm 130. You will never lose what God is giving you, by waiting upon the Lord for wisdom, and trusting in the Holy Spirit to lead and guide you in wise counsel and truth. It is very important these days not to exclude Dan from the family of Jacob, but to join and apply him in our life. Thank you.

I want to close out this chapter with another illustration from life. One day, a close relative of mine called me to tell me that my cousin was in the hospital and not expected to live. He was very ill and needed a visit from me to tell him about Jesus. So, I went to the hospital to visit with him. We talked for a few minutes about old times. I realized he was not able to talk very well for lack of breath and so, at that, I must move quickly on my mission. I began to talk to him about his soul, and about his need for salvation. He called the nurses and told them to get me out of his room and to not allow me back. But stubborn as I am, I came back the next day, and when I walked through the door, he called the nurses and told them to remove me again. This was not what I had expected. The next day, I went back to visit him again. He was more aggressive than ever and told me to get out of his room and leave him alone. I was heartbroken. Surely the Lord wanted him saved. Surely I was about my Father's business. I went home that day and began to inquire of the Lord, "Show me, Lord, what I have to do." The Lord gave me peace that it would be all right.

Three weeks later, I got a phone call. It was a Sunday afternoon, and it was from my cousin in the hospital. He said, "Edwin could you come and pray with me? I believe I need to bend my knee to the Lord, and ask Jesus to forgive me and come into my heart." I told him I would be there as quickly as I could get there. When I arrived, his wife and, I believe, four of his daughters were in the room. I closed the door and began to talk with my cousin. As I was getting ready to lead him through the Sinner's Prayer, I looked up at his wife and daughters and asked them, "Have you ever accepted the Lord as your Saviour and asked Him to be Lord of your life?" They indicated to me that they had not done this. I asked, "Would you like to join your dad and your husband today, and ask the Lord to forgive you of your sin, and invite Christ into your life as your Saviour?" They all said, "Yes. Yes." What a wonderful experience it was that day to lead that family to the Lord. The next day my cousin went to be with the Lord. I was with him when he passed and saw the smile on his face as he left this world. The lesson here: how to judge, how to wait upon the Lord, and how to respond in the midst of conflict or adversity and, yet, be available at the time of need to be used by the Lord.

Today I can say I thank the Lord so much for having gone through that experience but, I must confess, at the time it was not very pleasant. I share this with you because I believe you need to realize judgment does begin at the house of God. I believe that many people suffer needlessly and die outside the will of God, because the Church has not learned how to judge righteously. It is easier to say, "Do not judge," but that, my friend, is a judgment. The Kingdom of God is within us and we must allow it to be expressed through our lives, through our words, and through our example. People need to see Christ in you, which is their hope for glory. So let's bring Jesus to them. Amen.

CHAPTER 8

Christic Revealed

I n this chapter it is my hope to reveal more of the nature of Jesus Christ and answer these questions: who was He, when was He here on earth, and how is He in us today? Looking at a few Scriptures, we find an interesting question in John 9:10, 15, and 26—"Who did this to you?" This is the story of the blind man who was healed. The writer says, "But we see Jesus," and in Colossians 1:27 the writer says, "Christ in you, the hope of glory."

Looking at another Scripture in Revelation 21:10, John said, "And He carried me away in the spirit to a great and high mountain. He showed me that great City, the holy Jerusalem, descending out of heaven from God." We need a revelation that only the Holy Spirit can show us so that we can really see what is going on here.

What happened when John got the revelation? He became a worshipper. A person will only worship God if he sees God in something. In Matthew 28:17, after Jesus was resurrected, it says, "After they saw Him they worshipped

Him." The principle here is that we must have a vision and a revelation of who Christ is, in our spirit, in order to be a worshipper of Him. We learn here that when John saw these things, he became a worshipper. We know the story of the woman at the well who, after she had met Jesus, became a worshipper. It is interesting that when Moses got a revelation he worshipped, when Peter got a revelation of who Jesus was, he became a worshipper. In Acts 13, we read that as they worshipped, the Lord spoke. He revealed something. So our thoughts today, as we are reading this Book, let us do it in a spirit of worship and see what the Lord will reveal to us.

Jesus said, "I will build My Church." I feel that one of the reasons why the Church has not yet been built is that it does not really know who Jesus is; they really don't know who Jesus of the Bible really is. The whole book of Revelation was written under the direction of the Holy Spirit, for the express purpose of revealing who Jesus is, to the Church. First of all, the Church has to see Him. Then He will be visible to the world through the Church. This is how the Church will be built. I believe that JESUS is building His Church. It is a glorious thing.

The sons of Jacob did not know who Joseph was in Pharaoh's hall the first time they came, but when Benjamin was with them, Joseph revealed himself. Likewise, the Church will not know who Jesus is until the Church is fully engaged. In Revelation 21:10, it says, the Holy City, heavenly Jerusalem, was descending. Everybody today wants to ascend unto the heavens, while I see here that something is descending. When it says that the Holy City comes down, I do not believe that means in the geographical sense, but that it is coming from the

INVISIBLE REALM into the VISIBLE REALM. In Matthew 8:1 the Bible tells us that as Jesus descended from the mountain, great multitudes followed Him. In Revelation 21:10 we see a similar situation: the holy city descending. The same thing is happening here. God is opening His bosom and releasing Christ to the world. He is saying to the world, "This is what I am, this is Who I am; I am the love of God." Jesus is the love of God revealed. What we see when Jesus comes down from the mountain with the multitudes following Him, is the same thing we read about here in Revelation, as the City of God, the new Jerusalem, descends from heaven. Multitudes are following and this manifests the glory of God. As we continue to meditate on these truths, we will discover the beautiful truth that God Himself is our possession.

This points to an hour when many people who are interested in their dreams, their visions, and their possessions, I'm talking about Christians who are crying out to God and saying, if we can only have a New Testament Church. While we have many churches, they still seem to miss the visitations of God. He is still our possession, our protection, and our inheritance. I have an inheritance and it is in Him; He has an inheritance and it is in me. Here, the Bible is talking about the City that has possessed the glory or the nature of God. I also will have possessed Him but, much more importantly, He will have possessed me and, in the words of Solomon, "He is mine and I am His." If we could truly comprehend that we, as the people of God, are the City of God, then our reality is this—that we are the substance of the glory of God.

They cried out, "Sirs, we would see Jesus." Jesus replied: "I'll tell you how it's going to happen. I am the

Word. I am the seed, and My Father is going to plant Me in this earth, and I'm going to bring forth more just like Me. There is going to be a multiplication of Me to such an extent that, as in Antioch, they were seen as someone so Christ-like they called them Christians, and the people of the Way, they also took knowledge of the fact that they had been with Me." My hope is that there is enough evidence in my life to convict me of being a Christian. I want people to see Christ in me. It is hard to put into words what I feel in my heart and know what the City consists of. Like Martin Luther King Jr., I have a dream; I have a vision; I see it can be people who actually possess the glory of God and what is on God's heart that He wants them to do. The City has the nature of God, and the City has a light that is as clear as crystal, the colour of water.

Jesus said, "Out of man's belly will flow rivers of living water." This was when He spoke of the Holy Ghost. When He, the Spirit of truth is come, He will guide you into all truth. This Church that has the glory of God and the light that is as clear as crystal, the colour of water, begins to manifest the glory of God. We are going to see a people who are God-possessed. They will have the fullness of understanding, and they will be guided through these twelve Gates of experience and revelation into all truth.

This means that the eyes of our understanding will have been opened—not in the sense that we memorize the Scriptures, or that we will know what the Bible says, but we will begin to realize that truth is a Person. Pilate asked, "What is truth?" Jesus answered him and said, "I am truth." Truth is a Person. We deal with this a lot. Is truth something we do, or is it who we are? Jesus came from the bosom of the Father, and He was full of grace and truth. I believe that being filled with the Holy Spirit can be manifested through grace and truth.

Another thought on the glory of God being visible, is that He became tangible. The names of God, and the acts of God reveal the glory of God. When we see the acts of God being demonstrated, we are seeing the glory of God manifested. I believe these are inseparable. He is still Jehovah-TSIDKENU, the Lord my righteousness; He is still Jehovah-M'KADDESH, my sanctifier; He is still Jehovah-SHALOM, my peace; He is still Jehovah-SHAMMAH, the one who was there; He is still Jehovah-ROPHE, my healer; He is still Jehovah-JIREH, my provider; He is still Jehovah-NISSI, my banner; and He is still Jehovah-ROHI, my shepherd. God is Jehovah SABAOTH, THE LORD OF HOSTS. Every time that one of these things are manifested, God's glory is revealed. Someone said, "Susie has cancer." And that may be a fact, but truth says, "By My stripes, she is healed." We need to be able to let the invisible God become visible and heal her. We, who are called the children of God—which is the real Church of the Lord Jesus Christ—if so led by the Spirit of God, should be able to reveal the presence of God or the glory of God. For, as many who were led by the Spirit of God, they are the sons of God and they will be led and guided into what—all truth—and shall do exploits in His name.

Having the glory of God, having all truth, and being the light of God in the earth, speaks of the Holy Spirit in us, revealing the truth of God through us. John 16:13 tells us that when the Spirit of truth comes, He is going to lead us and guide us. Where?—into the City; into the truth. He is going to lead us through those Gates, those experiences, those revelations of the glory of God—which is the true expression of Christ in the Church, which is the nature of God in full measure, grace, and truth. So, I asked the question, "What good is it to be full of grace and truth, and the world not knowing?" Grace and truth are like a river demonstrating the presence of God. The grace of God can do no good unless it reaches its destination. Facts can still remain facts, until truth opens blind eyes and deaf ears, causes the dumb to speak, the lame to walk, the sick to be healed, and the dead to come to life. May God give us the grace to repent of unbelief. I believe that the glory of God is summed up in one word—Jesus. When the Greeks asked, "Sir, we would see Jesus." Can we answer them, "Heavenly Father, glorify Me with Your own self, that they may see You and know that You are here to visit with them?"

When we realize how Jesus was able to glorify the Father through His nature, I believe we can do that by revealing Christ through the nature of the Holy Spirit within us. This is an answer to the Lord's prayer over us. John 17:20-22 tells us Jesus prayed, saying, "I do not pray just for these disciples, but for those also which shall believe on Me through the word of the disciples; that they all may be one, as Thou, Father art in Me, and I in You; that they also may be one in us, that the world may believe that You have sent Me. And the glory which You gave Me, I have given them, that they may also give to those who follow them." Those that He called, He justified; and those that He justified, He glorified. I believe this is bigger than we have ever imagined. So, what is the purpose of us revealing the glory of God? That the world may be saved, set free from the power of sin and made well. There is going to be a Church, a City, a Bride—whatever your preference—that is going to be the exact image and likeness of Jesus Christ. As we look at Revelation 21:11, it says that the City has the glory of God in it. It has become the brightness of His glory and the expressed image of His person.

This message is going to cost you. This means total commitment, not occasional visits. These light ministries, or ministries of revelation, showing the Kingship of Jesus Christ, the high priestly ministry of Jesus, rulership in spiritual places, and the ministry of authority is going to cost you your life. Will a man lay down his life for his friends? As the Spirit of God rests upon the Church, the Spirit of wisdom, understanding, counsel, might and knowledge, and the fear of God rests upon us all. This is the life of Christ manifested through the Church. God does not dwell in a temple or a building made with hands. Daniel saw a vision of the stone being cut out of the mountain. This stone will smite the image that seems to be threatening the ministry God has called us to fulfill. As ministers of the truth, we must be able to stand before the Body of Christ and demonstrate what real love is all about. The stone Daniel saw is the perfected Church, indeed, the glory of God, or the nature of God, and the light of God. The light was the truth. The strength is going to smite the image that would try to threaten the work of God. The weapons of our warfare are not carnal but mighty to the pulling down of strongholds. When the Spirit of truth is come, He will lead and guide us into all truth and, while He is doing that, He will be smiting the image and the imaginations that would try to exalt themselves against God. The Holy Spirit is teaching us how to handle the presence of God, without harshness, and not in bitterness, but being able to speak the truth in love as we do this.

We will see these worlds, denominations, doctrines of devils and all their isms, their philosophies. Everything they have built that is not of God, will be broken. I say, "Lord, smite or break this image in me," and as He does this, I see my own life becoming a praise to God, a beacon of hope, a light in the dark place. Even though we have feet of clay, we still stand between the iron hand of communism and the clay of democracy, the iron hand of Roman Catholicism and the clay of Pentecost. We need to get on our knees and ask God to show us what to do.

One Sunday morning, as I was speaking in the church in Dartmouth, the Lord spoke to me. He said, "The paradigm is shifting." This was back in 1993. I had no understanding of that word or what it meant. It was not in my vocabulary. Only now am I beginning to understand some of the things God was trying to show me. Leadership is going to change. The type of leaders God needs to build His Church, to run the administration of the Church, to declare His presence in the Church, to change the Church to what is presently seen as full-time ministers of the Gospel of the Kingdom, from weekend preachers and conference speakers, to people who spend their time in fellowship with God, listening for His voice and being willing to sacrifice everything they are asked by the Lord, and to be obedient to His Word. I can see that the paradigm has already shifted. This is why I feel this book and this message is so important right now. We have the authority to rule over principalities and powers when we have God in our hearts. Jesus Christ needs to be in our lives, in our inward parts, and we must believe this truth.

If the same Spirit that raised Christ from the dead dwells in us, He will quicken our mortal bodies and make us aware that He is present. Then, we must be willing to allow Christ to come forth by the Holy Spirit to accomplish His will through us, not just by the will of man, but by the will of God.

One Saturday night, at about 1:00 a.m., I had a phone call. I thought it was a prank, but I answered it anyway. It was a surgeon from the hospital. He asked me my name and verified who I was. I asked him who he was, and he told me he was a surgeon in the hospital and gave me his name. I still thought he was joking and then he said, "Sir, I have a man here who is bleeding to death. He has been stabbed, and unless the bleeding stops he will die. He has your card in his pocket and he has asked us to call you. He is scared to death that if he dies he will go to hell. Could you come and see him?" I said I would. So I got up and dressed. It was about a twenty mile drive.

I arrived at the hospital and the security guards at the door were expecting me. They hurried me up to the operating room, scrubbed me down, gave me a gown, and hurried me to his bedside. Here was a man weighing about 260 pounds, 6 foot 3 inches tall, with six—yes, six—stab wounds in his back. Each time his heart beat, you could see the blood rise. It was not squirting out, but it was just oozing out a little bit. It was not a pretty sight. I bent over to his head and introduced myself. He was whimpering; there was not a lot of strength left in this big man. He asked, "Can you help me?" I said, "Maybe Jesus can." He said, "I hope so." Then, he asked, "Am I going to go to hell?" I said, "You don't have to. You can give your heart to Jesus right now and put your life in His hands, and He will help you." The doctors were working on him, trying to slow down the blood flow and I was praying the Sinner's Prayer with him. When I finished, his whimpering turned into a sob and he thanked me for coming. When I looked up the doctors were looking at him and the blood had stopped flowing. It was a miracle. They were able to sew him up and make him comfortable. Before I left, he asked me if I would take his clothes and wash them, and bring them back to him tomorrow. I told him I would. I will never forget looking at his jacket, holding it up to the light and seeing those six knife holes in the back.

I could not come to see him the next day, which was Sunday, but I came in on Monday. The clothes were clean and I was hoping he would still be there to wear them. He was happy to see me but he was very concerned. The police were going to arrest him and put him in jail for assault and battery. He was able to explain to me what had happened. He had come home for the weekend from working out on an oil rig off the coast, and found his wife with another man. He removed the man from his house and, in the process of doing that, his wife stabbed him in the back six times. He recovered quickly, and they removed him from the hospital and took him to the jail. I made arrangements to come and visit him in jail and to do a Bible study with him. I visited with him two and, sometimes, three times a week. He was there for six weeks and, during that time, he was reunited with his wife and family. All was forgiven. Their family was now established in Christ and a true commitment was made to the Lord.

I feel so honoured to have been called upon by the Lord to be involved in this situation, and to be able to tell the story as one who has seen and heard the Lord in a very special way. Before I meet this man and his family in heaven, I pray that I may see them here on earth. I think that would be a great day. This is a true case where his friends came and asked him, "Who did this to you?" First the stabbing, second that healing, third the restoration, and he told them, "It was Jesus." He said the Lord visited him in his darkest hour and gave him hope, and as he looked towards the Church, his body was healed, his marriage restored, his sins forgiven, and his life was changed forevermore. Yes, Jesus did this. I look at this and I can truly say I have seen the Lord. I have seen the hand of God move swiftly in a very miraculous way to save this man's life and his family. I believe it is things like this that the Church needs to become familiar with, in order to really and truly be the hand of God extended, the life of God revealed, and the presence of God manifested. It is my deepest conviction that people need the Lord. Amen.

CHAPTER 9

That I Might Know Him

From the very beginning of this book, it has been my deepest desire to reveal to you what Jesus Christ means to me. First of all, I would like to say that the more I study, and the more I learn about Jesus, the more I desire to not only do the things that He did, but to get to know Him more intimately every day.

It has become one of the greatest revelations to me to be able to hear the Lord's voice, and to understand what He is trying to say, not only to me but to the Church. The process the Lord has led me to use to hear His voice and to understand what He is saying means having a committed **prayer life**. As I mentioned earlier, the Lord has used some of His great teachers in the Body of Christ to teach others of us the knowledge of God's Word and how to really pray it effectively. The words the disciples said, "Lord, teach us to pray like You do," have meant so much to me. I have found that you cannot always just throw any old thing out there in prayer and expect God to respond to it. **Prayer is a commitment.** It means sacrifice; it means perseverance. Not just, "Hello, Lord. How are You doing?" Yes, it is much more than that. We read in Hebrews 4:2 that the Gospel was preached to the Jews but it did not profit them because they did not mix it with faith. Verses 7-10 tell us that today after such a long time, if you will hear His voice and harden not your hearts, you will be able to enter into the rest of God. Furthermore, in verse 16 we read, *"Let us therefore come boldly unto the throne of grace, that we may obtain mercy, and find grace to help in times of need."* This has become one of my guiding Scriptures—hearing God's voice and learning to obey it, that I might be able to help others who are not hearing and do not know what they are to obey, and so that they may also enjoy the mighty presence of God.

I want to share some more stories with you and events that took place in our ministry that helped to form what I believe, and gave my faith some form of substance. These things I am sharing are examples of what happens when you mix your faith with the Word of God—something incredible can take place. A great teacher of the Word said, "Bread will do you no good until you eat it." Jesus told us that He is the Bread of Life; He is the bread that came down from heaven. Jesus told the disciples, "This is my body which has been broken for you. Take, eat all of it." This is not intended to be a book on theology, or on correcting those that are wrong and those that are right, but a book of my experience of living in Christ.

Let's glance back at the twelve sons of Jacob, where we find Naphtali the eighth son of Jacob, whose name means "wrestler." There is a lot of truth that we as Christians wrestle with. We wrestle with the process. We wonder so much about why this happened and why that happened, what this means and what that means. Someone once said that the answer is always simple when found. Sometimes when we are wrestling with truth, the answer is usually not too far away; quite often it is when we give up, that we realize the answer was right there. I think of Jacob the night he wrestled all night with the angel. It was only as he was leaving in the morning that he realized the Lord was there. Many times it is the same with us as we wrestle, not against flesh and blood, but against principalities and powers. We overcome them by the blood of the Lamb and the word of our testimony. I have tried to bring some understanding to revelation by my experience, hoping to help others who are going through the same struggles I have faced. I am often reminded by the Lord that it is His Church He is building, not mine, and that I need to listen to Him, not to my circumstances, or the needs that surround me. I need to be able to hear His voice, by His Spirit.

Some things that have caused me great concern is hearing people talking about a "sacred ground." What really is holy ground? We do not worship the earth; we must worship God and Him only. Also, when I hear things like "You need to be baptized to be saved," I recall two events that came into my life that consumed a lot of my time, only to realize afterwards, they were a waste. God will judge these people, so leave that to Him.

Here is just a little description of what I am talking about: our small church group had approached another church group who owned a campground on a nice little lake. We had made arrangements with them to have a weekend with our men, where we could go and pray and have fellowship with one another and with the Lord. On the very day we were leaving to go to the campground, the owner of the campground called me and told me they could not allow us on the property. I asked him why. He explained to me that this was sacred ground committed to the Lord's service, and because we spoke in other tongues, we could not be permitted on the property. To this very day, I find that so very hard to understand. I have prayed many times for the Lord to bring understanding, either to them or to me, because what he was saying was very wrong to us. We found another place, so we were able to go and enjoy the presence of the Lord, and we had a great time. If you have an understanding of this I would be glad to hear from you.

On another occasion, I had a young man come to us. He was devastated. He explained what had happened to him. He and his family were attending a church in our town; they had been going there for two years, and the leadership finally consented to them getting saved. In order to do that they needed to be baptized in water, to which they agreed. On the day of their baptism, this young man was baptized twelve times. He was supposed to come up out of the water speaking in other tongues. It never happened and, as a result of him not receiving the gift of tongues, he and his family were escorted to the door and were told that God had refused them. They were excommunicated and so they left, not knowing where to turn. They came to us, so broken, asking if this was possible. We were able to show this couple how God loved them, that Jesus died on the cross for their sin, and all they needed to do was believe this and they would be saved. These are just two of the examples of weird stuff being taught out there in the world as some form of Christianity.

These people also believe they are hearing from God. I believe this is what Paul was referring to when he said to avoid the doctrines of devils.

Now, I want to tell you about a few more events that took place in our ministry that demonstrate the great lengths God will go to for one lost sinner. Here we see the story in the Bible about the Shepherd who left the ninety-nine and went out and found the one lost sheep and brought it into the fold. 1 Peter 2 tells us that there is going to be a people in the earth made in the image of God. For every high priest taken from among men, God is going to apprehend you; He is going to reach into your family, your church, and into your job and get you. He will reveal Himself to you, so that you will know who He is, and who it is that truly apprehended you. In John 15:16, Jesus said, *"Ye have not chosen me, but I have chosen you, and ordained you, that ye should go and bring forth fruit."* No man can take this honour unto himself; it is God who calls and it is God who ordains to bring forth fruit.

It was a Sunday afternoon, and we had just finished watching a television program that was on the local television channel. The name of the show was called "Jesus Now," and we were on every Sunday afternoon and every Thursday night. It was a program where people would give their testimony and share how God had saved them and how their lives had changed. It was wonderful to know you could get saved and be kept by the Lord. On this particular Sunday afternoon, just as the program ended, I received a call from an elderly gentleman, asking, "How do I know if I am born again?" To which I replied, "I'd be happy to tell you." Of course, I shared the Scriptures with him, and he asked me if I would come to his house and explain this to him and his wife, to which I agreed.

On Monday, Denise and I went to visit them. At the door of a beautiful home, he met us and escorted us straight into his wife's bedroom. It was almost the size of our house. She was laying there in the bed, propped up on the pillows, seemingly very comfortable. Her first statement to me was, "We watched your program and we are wondering what we must do to be saved?" I started to share from Acts 16:30-31. The gentleman interrupted me and began to explain that they had gone to church in this particular denomination for forty-five years and hardly ever missed a Sunday. He was a part of just about every program the church offered, yet they were told you cannot know for sure if you are saved. I can only tell you that my heart sank when I heard that statement.

They shared that they had been to the Mayo Clinic outside of Boston and could not get any more medical help. They were told to go home. His wife had very little time left—maybe months. These were very difficult times for them; they were very wealthy. It was easy to see that the gentleman took such loving care of his wife, with so much compassion. Not knowing if they were saved, seemed their greatest concern. The Lord led me to take them for a walk down the Romans Road. If you are a Christian you know what I mean. The anointing of God was there and the Lord's presence could be felt. They received every word I shared with tears of joy. This lady had been in this bed for a number of years with liver cancer, knowing that any day might be her last on this earth, and wondering what they had to do to know they were saved. We were able, by the beautiful grace of God, to share with them the

Scriptures and bring them to a knowledge of salvation. Great joy was celebrated in that household that day!

As we were leaving the house and walking out to the car, the Lord spoke to me. He said, "Bring Communion here tomorrow and celebrate Communion with them." The next day, we put our little Communion package together and went and knocked on the door. They were surprised but very glad to see us. They invited us in and asked, "What brings you back today?" I explained to them that we were there to celebrate Communion with him and his wife. The Lord had spoken to me when leaving yesterday that I was to do this. The gentleman quickly told me that they were not good enough to celebrate Holy Communion. So, without being too critical as to why, we set up our Communion service. We taught them from the Scriptures just what Communion was and why we should do this. The Spirit of the Lord was upon us; it was awesome. We broke bread together, sharing from the Scriptures that this was not because we were good enough, but that Jesus makes us good enough. We had some more conversation and we left rejoicing. They were so happy to know that they were good enough to fellowship with the Holy Spirit, the Lord Jesus Christ, and their Heavenly Father, not because of what they had done, but because of what Christ had done for them on the cross of Calvary.

I tell you this story because I had never seen an elderly couple so happy. As we were leaving the house that day the Lord spoke to me again. He said, "I want you to come back tomorrow and ask the lady to bring her sisters to visit with her." I thought that was kind of strange, but if the Lord wanted me to do it, I would.

So the next day, we went and knocked on the door again. The gentleman was very surprised and with a chuckle he said, "My, oh my, what brings you today?" I told him the Lord had told me to come and to tell his wife that she should bring her sisters to visit with her. I said, "I sure hope she has some sisters." He laughed and then shook his head and went into the bedroom to his wife and told her what we had just said. We could hear her exclaim, "Never, never, never, never!" He came out to speak with us. We asked if we could go and speak with his wife ourselves. I asked her, "Do you have any sisters?" She said, "Yes, yes I have three." I said, "Ma'am, I did not know this; therefore, I believe that the Lord wants you to see your sisters. We must do this. Why, might I ask, do you not want to see them?" She said, "I want them to remember me when I was beautiful, before this disease has destroyed my life." I said. "Regardless," and I called her by name, "we have to get your sisters and have them come to the house." She resisted and I persisted. I asked, "Where do they live?" She told me. They were all within a couple of miles. I thought, "How sad." I instructed her husband to go and get those ladies and bring them here; we would wait until he returned. He took about an hour, and when those four ladies saw each other, all in their September years, it is a scene I will never forget as long as I live. I think I sang, "Thank You, Lord" for days; it was so beautiful.

My thoughts: How could a church be so cruel to teach such lies? How could the devil blind people's mind to the truth? Could this really be true? If we had not witnessed it ourselves, it would be hard to believe. That lady should have died several years earlier because of the nature of her disease, according to the Mayo Clinic. I believe it was because they were asking God for answers, and God is so faithful that He spared her life, so that He could reveal Himself to her in the truth about salvation and Holy Communion. God also restored her relationship with her family, so that she could leave this earth in peace. She passed away and went to be with the Lord a few short months after this event. Praise the Lord.

My next story is just as profound as any I have told you before. One Saturday morning, Denise and I were having breakfast at our house. We had been listening to the early morning news, and the person on the radio was explaining a very terrible situation that had just taken place last evening in our city. A young man drove his car down one of the streets and side-swiped a whole bunch of police cruisers that had been parked in front of the precinct. From there, he drove about two more miles up onto the center of the Angus L. McDonald Bridge, stopped his car, and planned to jump over the side and end it all. However, the police had caught up to him, and a policeman grabbed him by the tail of his coat just as he was about to leap over the side. He was able to rescue the young man from taking his life. I said to Denise, "Let us pray for that young man; I believe that Jesus can help him," and so we did.

Within minutes, the phone rang and there was a young man on the phone. He seemed anxious. He asked me my name to make sure he had the right person. He said, "I don't know you, but I have heard about you. Have you been listening to the news?" I told him we had just listened to a terrible report about a young man who almost jumped off the bridge. He said the young man was his very close friend. "He is going through a very difficult time and he needs a lot of help. Would you help him? The police have taken him to the Nova Scotia Hospital for an assessment, and I was wondering if you could go and see him, and maybe pray for him." We said we would do that. He gave me the particulars I needed—the young man's name and where he was in the hospital.

We were able to visit with him and share the wonderful knowledge of salvation and grace that was available to him from the Lord Jesus Christ. To see that young man's face light up in that den of iniquity was just incredible. To make a long story short, this young man was a car detailer. He was one of the best in the business, but he had a problem with drugs and alcohol. These were consuming his life, and he decided on this particular evening, that it was time to end it all. He had a wife and two small children. This was a really sad situation.

After some time, he was able to get out of the institution and stay at home while he was being further assessed. He was allowed to come and visit us at the church. We were constructing the church building at the time, and he would come every day and work with us on the construction. There he was able to interact with the brethren while we were building and working together every day. He was able to see Christianity in real action. We were able to develop a relationship with him and his family. They came to our fellowship for a while and were restored in body, soul, and spirit. Eventually, they moved back to Ontario to live.

It still amazes me how quickly the Lord answered our prayer, and how quickly this young man was delivered from his addictions and sinful nature, and brought into a relationship with the Lord, where he could have peace with himself and enjoy his family. It is my strong conviction, that this is one of the responsibilities of the Church of Jesus Christ that seems to be overlooked. There are many people today who are being treated for mental illness when, in fact, they are demon-possessed. The Church can deliver these people where the doctors cannot, and neither can medicine. It is my prayer that all Christians everywhere would see this. The reason for putting this story in this book is that, when the Church becomes more aware of who they are in Christ, and of some of the things that can be done in the name of Jesus through the ministry we have been given, more action will be taken. Ask the Lord to use you in these areas. You need not be afraid, because the Lord is with you; He has not given you the spirit of fear, but of love, power, and a sound mind. Share what you have with those who need what you have. Amen.

I believe that it is imperative that Christians start having conversations with the Lord about what the Lord would have them do. I find that this helps to get your mind off yourself and onto others and, when you truly get this, you will be amazed at what God will do through you. You will soon realize how exciting life can really be as a servant of the Most High God.

I want to share a couple more stories with you. One day, I was in the hospital visiting with a friend and, as I was coming out of the elevator, a lady came up towards me screaming at the top of her voice, "You must come and help me." I had never seen this lady before, and I had no idea what was happening. She kept on insisting, "Come, come, come!" She kept on telling me, and then she took hold of my arm. So I got on the elevator with her. She seemed to know where she was going. She told me that her son was having surgery. We went down to the recovery ward, where she began pleading with the doctors and nurses to allow me to go in and pray with her son. He had just gone through major surgery and she wanted me to pray for him, that God would heal him. As we were talking, the nurses wheeled him past us on a gurney. This lady became hysterical and had to be restrained by the nurses. Finally, they told her that her son could only have one visitor and that would be me or herself. She insisted, "Let this man go and pray for him." And they agreed.

They brought me into the recovery room. I had no idea what this young man had been operated on for, or any knowledge of what was really going on with him, but I went by faith to pray for him that God would heal him. He was only nineteen years old, and he had just gone through lymph gland surgery. He looked a mess. After I had prayed for him, I left the hospital with his mother and she thanked me so much. She was so appreciative. Just to spare you details, she had seen me on television.

Three days later, I went into the hospital to visit my friend again and also this young man I had prayed for. When I got to his room, he was sitting on the side of his bed wanting to go home. The doctors were with him and they could not believe that he was healed and able to leave the hospital so soon. So they checked him over thoroughly. It was a time of great celebration for his mother and his young wife. It was hard to believe the miracle that had just taken place. We were able to get him a place to stay, and got him connected with a church that was next door to where he was now living. I knew the pastor there, and I knew he would help this young man if anyone could.

Everything seemed to be going along fine for several months and then, one day, I got a call from his mother.

Unfortunately, she had bad news. He had overdosed. I could not believe it. She asked me to take his funeral. This had to be one of the saddest situations that any mother or wife could ever possibly have to face. There were so many questions with no answers it seemed. This was one tough funeral. There was a lot of sorrow, sadness, and grief over this situation. I was taken to the passage in Matthew 12:43-45 which talks about when the unclean spirit is gone out of a man, the spirit walks through dry places seeking rest. When it doesn't find any, he then says, "I will return to the house from whence I came," and finds it empty, swept, and garnished. Then he goes and takes with him seven other spirits more wicked than himself, and they enter in and dwell in the house. The last state of that man is worse than the first. It is hard to understand how someone who could have been delivered and healed by God, could possibly go back to that old way of life and escape. Folks, the devil is a liar, and we must tell people that are going through these situations what their options are. Come to Jesus and He will heal you, He will save you, He will restore your hope, and be your help. Do not walk away from Him. But if you do, know that there are consequences. The devil is like a roaring lion, roaming up and down the earth looking for someone to devour. Church, stop him in his tracks, and let him go no further in the name of Jesus. Amen.

I have one more story I want to tell you, before I bring this chapter to a close. We were living on the south shore of Nova Scotia, in a little village called Chester. We had been called there to minister in a small church. It was a beautiful seaside village, steeped in marine history. One day, Denise and I decided to drive around the neighbouring communities to become familiar with our new surroundings. We came to a three-way stop, and while I was stopped and looking around to see if anything was coming, I heard the Lord speak to me. He said, "I have a church here. I need you to bless it." So we looked up and down the road; we looked all over the place, and there was no church building in sight. "Oh well," I thought, "maybe it was something the Lord wants to show me," and left it at that. So I prayed about it and left it with the Lord.

On the following Sunday morning, a new couple arrived at church, and they had some children with them. We met with them after the service, introducing ourselves, and making the usual welcoming commentary. I asked them where they were from and they told me they were from a little village not too far away. They described the very place where the Lord had told me He had a church, which we could not find. They invited us to come to their house. They wanted to meet with us and we did. When we arrived at the house they were so glad to see us. We were welcomed and made to feel at home. I noticed that the walls were full of pictures. I mean totally full of pictures. They called it their "wall of fame." I could not help but mention to them that they had so many pictures of children, to which they responded, "We are foster parents and we have raised fifty-four children. We have had six weddings in our family and there could be more. The Lord has blessed us with the gift of parenting. We take these children and we raise them for Jesus." They said, "We have our own little church here." I was so impressed, and as I thought about it, the Lord reminded me, "You have not seen a church like this before." It was then that I understood what the Lord meant that day when He told me He had a church in that community.

More and more, every day, I realize how important it is that we learn to hear the voice of the Lord, and know that it is Him, so that we can be more effective in ministry when He calls upon us to do some more building with Him. We are co-labourers with the Lord, and I share these experiences because I do not believe that I should take memories like these to heaven with me. Maybe somebody could be encouraged to keep on keeping on if they heard them.

I want to close this chapter on a positive note. We should not be alarmed when these things become visible. Jesus warns us in the Scriptures, *"Beware of false prophets who come to you in sheep's clothing, but inwardly they are ravenous wolves. You will know them by their fruits"* (Matthew 7:15-16, NKJV). The Lord says, *"Not everyone who says to Me, 'Lord, Lord,' shall enter the kingdom of heaven, but he who does the will of My Father in heaven"* (verse 22, NKJV). Later in Matthew 7:24-25 we read: *"Whoever hears these sayings of Mine, and does them, I will liken him to a wise man who built his house on the rock [and when the winds and the storms come they will stand firm]"* (NKJV). Paul warned Timothy that in the last days difficult times would come, and gives a list of things that will have to be dealt with, that are all rooted in sin. He said these people will have a form of godliness, but will have no power, so he should avoid them. They will be ever learning and never able to come to the knowledge of the truth. Remember who is truth—Jesus said I am the way, the truth, and the light.

As we look at the story of Jacob again, we see Joseph, who is a type of Christ. He speaks of being a preserver of life, one who will bring together the family of God, bringing them to that place of repentance, and finding peace with God, our Heavenly Father. Benjamin is the full brother of Joseph; his name means "the son of my right hand." Benjamin, I believe, is a type of the Church, and Joseph is a type of Christ. Today as we study Joseph, Benjamin, and their brothers, we see where God brought them altogether at the end. They did eventually wind up in Canaan, the land of milk and honey.

One has to ask the question, "Could there be a more dysfunctional family anywhere?" This can surely give us a picture of the Church today. It gives me great hope that there is a great life yet to be lived on this earth in serving the Lord Jesus Christ. Remember, Jesus is coming for a spotless Bride, with no spots, no wrinkles. There is a double blessing here—being blessed of God in salvation, healing, and deliverance, and being able to demonstrate that to people who do not know who Jesus is. This, my friends, is our mandate. We have a message from God to the world that Jesus loves them. He gives us the power to do things in His name, such as the stories that I have shared with you. These things can only happen if God is in it, with the Holy Spirit releasing His power to accomplish these things. I believe that we can truly say, "It is no longer I that liveth, but Christ who now lives in me. The life that I now live in the flesh I live by faith in the Son of God, who loved me and delivered Himself up for me"— which is Christ in you, the hope of glory.

CHAPTER 10

Jesus in the Church

It has been as hard to bring this book to a close as it was to get it started. As I mentioned at the beginning, the Lord had spoken to me about studying the twelve sons of Jacob. My question to the Lord at that time was, "What should I look for? What is the most significant thing I need to be aware of in order to make sense of this whole exercise?" I had read so many books, talked to so many wonderful people, and gathered so much information that I did not know where to start. So after twenty-plus years, I have yielded to the calling of the Holy Spirit to write these things down so that others may run with it. I have learned over the years that we can learn from our mistakes, but it is less painful and more beneficial to learn from the mistakes of others. In order to do that, we must learn to listen, learn to observe, and also, learn to discern. I have shared many things with you—things that have broken my heart, and have taken me into the heavenlies. So, now with God's grace at work in my life, I would like to try and bring this to a close.

When the Lord first laid this on my heart, I had never read anything about the twelve sons of Jacob. But then, when I started to research this topic, I found that there are many other books out there on this subject. I asked the Lord, "What is it that you want me to say?" And I believe this is the main message: the importance of not dwelling on our circumstances, but learning to listen to the Lord.

The twelve gates into the Holy City are like twelve pearls, and each one of these pearls is a separate, personal identification. There should be no confusion as to which gate we are looking at. The one thing I noticed, is that every pearl is formed the same way: a grain of sand gets in the oyster and irritates and irritates until it produces the beautiful pearl. Experience, without a revelation, is a waste of time. The thing I have discovered, is that God gives us revelation, and as we try to gain understanding we have many experiences. Many times our experiences are irritating, to say the least, but if we stay with it and continue to pray about it, I believe God has His hand in this. We will find that weeping may endure for a night but joy comes in the morning.

I have discovered that if you are in the ministry of preaching the Gospel of Jesus Christ, you had better be called of God to do so, or your frustrations will overtake you. On the other hand, if God has called you, your frustrations will build layers and layers of wisdom and knowledge—thus the forming of the pearl of great price. It is a testimony of the goodness of God in your life, and how He has brought you through all your experiences by the revelation of Jesus Christ. I found it interesting that the gates were all pearls, yet no two were alike, much like the children of Israel's twelve sons—none were similar. My experience, gained through the revelation of the Word to me, may not be quite the same as the way you heard and understood what God was saying to you. The key is that you heard and were able to understand. Another key is we all have the same Father—our Heavenly Father—who has the same purpose in mind for all of us; we are predestined for His glory, and to reveal Him to a world of sinners who do not know Him.

Many Christians come to Christ and experience the wonderful joy of meeting Jesus, having our sins forgiven, and a vision of hope eternal that, when we die, we will go to heaven and live with Jesus forever. Many of us Christians get saved, receive the baptism in the Holy Spirit, and some would believe that now they have it all— "The Kingdom of God is within me. I am without fear or intimidation." So we move out into the world in our new-found faith, declaring the lordship of Jesus Christ, and what we expected to happen does not take place. Frustrated, we start questioning our faith, and our walk with the Lord, wondering "Where did we miss it?" Maybe you have not had that experience, so I say, "The Lord bless you real good." But sometimes, as someone said, "No pain, no gain." You do not really realize how valuable something is in life until you lose it. Sometimes, things are lost and never found. We need to cherish the things of God as though our life depends on it, because it does.

I want to focus on Joseph and Benjamin in a little more depth, so our experience in Christ may seem a little more relevant. Both Joseph and Benjamin are a type of overcomer, who have been sent ahead of their brethren to preserve life, much like how Christ came to earth and gave His life that we might share that life with others to preserve them and give them hope. I believe that in the Old Testament we have the covenant of Law; in the New Testament we have a covenant of grace; and in Jesus Christ we have the example of how the Law and grace work together—one must be fulfilled before the other can be established.

As we look at the twenty-first chapter of Revelation there are so many things we need to consider, so I will just draw your attention to some of them. The twelve sons are twelve gates that allow one to enter into this City of God. We come from each side with different experiences, but we wind up in the City after having gone through the gates. Many people or church groups have come to one or more of these gates and camped out on the city walls, living on the fringes of Christianity instead of dining at the Master's table. It is God's will that we experience every revelation He releases to the Body of Christ. This may sound complicated, but it really isn't, because the Lord leads us. He knows how to get there if we will learn how to follow. I am just going to go through these twelve experiences which I believe are revelations to the Church, which the Holy Spirit is explaining to every believer. Like Paul said, we no longer have to live in ignorance.

We need to be born again (Reuben); we need to receive the baptism in the Holy Spirit (Simeon); we need to get involved in spiritual ministry (Levi); we need to learn how to praise the Lord and realize how important that is (Judah). We need to understand that the Gospel is free. Yes, it is not inexpensive, but it can't be bought (Issachar). We must be willing to identify with the Body of believers in Christ (Zebulun), to learn that overcoming the things of this world is done by the strength we have in Christ (Dan).

We must realize that we have been predestined to be conformed to the image of Christ (Gad); we must also learn to be content in every circumstance (Asher), believing that Christ is in charge of our lives and is a good lifestyle manager (Naphtali); we also need to realize that the Lord will add all that is necessary for us to have, seeking first the Kingdom of God and all these things He would give to you (Joseph); and last of all, we need to realize we are the Church (Benjamin).

We are not a sorrowful bunch or a hopeless crowd, but we are God's right hand here on this earth. All of these things are part of the believer's life and at the end of the day we can truly say, "God was with me all the way." When we study the life of Joseph, we will learn that all of these things were part of his experience. We will also learn, through the Gospels, that all of these things were our Lord's experience; and, lastly, as we study Paul's letters, we will see that he experienced all these things in his life. Now, I believe that it is the Church's turn to experience and demonstrate these things. In Revelation 3:21, the Bible tells us the overcomer will be granted *"to sit with me in my throne, even as I also overcame and am set down with my Father in his throne"* (NKJV). That, my friends, is a very powerful statement and a major promise from the Lord.

When we pass through all of these gates, with Benjamin being the last gate, we should find ourselves in the throne room of God. What does that mean? There we will know the presence of God. We will understand the presence of God. We will desire the presence of God. We will see that we need the presence of God, and that we will not want to be away from His presence for any reason at all.

If we lived every day of our lives believing that God is as close to us as our breath, I promise you, life would be a lot different. The fact is, that is the way it is. God is in our circumstances and, make no mistake about it, He is trying to produce in us a vessel that will demonstrate His glory.

One of the big problems is that nobody wants to wait; we are in such a hurry for the prize that we hate the process. There is a reason that Rachel is barren. Yes, we look at some churches and we do not see the manifestation of God by His Spirit. There are many times in our own church where we would like to experience more of the Pentecostal power than we do. Caution here: don't let barrenness condemn you; neither let it be an excuse for not reproducing. God wants Rachel to bring forth children of the Kingdom, but not until she stops envying her sisters. Trying to be like that church down the road, or better than that church down the road because you think you deserve better, are wrong attitudes. God is sovereign and He will, in the fullness of time, cause you to produce that ministry of purpose that He put you on this earth for. The challenge here is to be content where you are, calling upon the Lord every day and making yourself available, trusting the Lord for the outcome.

Many churches today, I believe, are in the place that Rachel was. She cried out saying, "Give me children or else I will die." As we look at the majority of churches today, there are no children, and this should cause us great alarm. It says in Genesis 30:22 that God remembered Rachel. It was God's timing. He opened her womb and she conceived and bore a son and said, "God has taken away my reproach." She called his name "Joseph," meaning,

"May the Lord give me another son." And Benjamin was the fulfillment of that prophecy.

Benjamin was a full brother to Joseph. They were both sons of Jacob that were born from the woman he loved. All of his other sons seem to have been born out of necessity, while awaiting the day that love would be manifested in the beginning to bring many sons to glory. Benjamin represents a type of the Church, as Joseph is a type of Christ. They are full brothers, and all the other brothers are half-brothers. This speaks of a 100% ministry, not 30%. Not 60%, but 100%.

This is why I believe it is important that we are willing to allow the Holy Spirit to take us through every one of these experiences. There will always be the harlot Church (a religious system that will draw you away from God), that will try to get you before you are ready; but we must be willing to wait on the Lord and hear His voice, which I have tried to emphasize all the way through this book. We must learn to recognize the voice of God without a doubt, or we will be sidetracked.

It is very tempting to boast of the things God is doing in your life. It takes a strong discipline to wait until the Lord tells you it is time to tell your story. You may sit in a prison house for fourteen years, but the day will come when the Lord will call you out and use you. You may have been misunderstood, you may be lied about or falsely accused, but God is very much aware of what is going on. Remember, He gave you the dream, He gave you the vision, He clothed you in His righteousness, and He will never forsake you. He has not forgotten you and He has not forgotten where you are. Be careful who you tell your dreams and visions to; they may not be the people you think they are. Be wise as a serpent and harm-less as a dove.

When God begins to move in your life people will call you exclusive. Do not pay any attention to what they say. The fruit of your ministry speaks for you. Sometimes you will have to let things in your life die; in other words, you may have to let go of some of the things you have been taught over the years that you believed as absolute truth. You may face death experiences, times of great wrestling; you may walk with a limp the rest of your life. When people ask you why you are limping, you can tell them the truth.

There will be times when you will feel like the Son of Sorrows, but trust me, God has a plan for your life. God is raising up a people who will die to self, like Rachel. When she gave birth to Benjamin, it cost her her very life. We read in Scripture that, as her soul was departing, in travail she brought forth Benjamin. God tells us in Isaiah, "Will I bring to the point of birth and not give birth?" In order for ministry to be complete, we must be willing to let go of the past and move on; all things will pass away and all things will be new.

The Church as we know it, is going to die, because it is soulish. It functions from the things it feels and sees—cir-cumstances, environment, etc.—and none of these things require faith. It functions without seeking the Lord for His direction and putting it into action. In order for the Benjamin ministry to come forth, the soul will have to die. The Church of Jesus Christ is a spiritual thing not a soulish thing. We must learn how to put off things that are carnal and learn to walk in the Spirit. The Bible tells us that if you are born of the Spirit, you must walk in the Spirit. It seems that most of the Church today likes to talk about Jesus, but do they allow Jesus to talk with them? Everybody wants the Lord, but are they willing to be like Him? The Word became flesh and dwelt among us and we beheld His glory. The Church is going to be known as the Son of God's right hand, whether we like it or not.

Many people ask me when I talk about these things, "Where is this Benjamin, 'the Church'?" My answer: It is hidden with Christ in God, preserved for purpose until the fullness of time. There is a generation of people right now, going to churches everywhere, who have never had a supernatural experience with the Lord. I believe this is about to change. Those that hunger and thirst after righteousness will be fed. One of the main purposes of the Church in the world today, is to verify the Word that became flesh and dwelt amongst us.

Benjamin is that ministry that is getting the Bride ready; it is the ministry of pioneering, a ministry of preserving life, preparing a bride to meet her groom. There are those today who are longing to see the face of Jesus. However, if they are not part of the Church of Jesus Christ, He will not reveal Himself to them. We have a type here in Genesis 43:1-3: "You will never see my face," said Joseph, "unless Benjamin is with you." To see Him is to be like Him. When God calls you away to be with Him, you cannot play the charismatic games any longer. This is not a theme park like Wonderland, on our way to Canaan that is to be in Christ. We are carrying the bones of Joseph. He said, "I want to be buried in Canaan." If we really want to be part of the living, moving, breathing Body of Christ, we are going to have to consider ourselves dead to self. God has a predestined purpose for us. We are encompassed with the tremendous cloud of witnesses and, somewhere in the grandstand of time, there is a midwife (prophetic voice/prophet) saying, "You will have this ministry also." Jesus said, "Greater things than I have done you will do." These words have always been a major challenging thought to me. I believe that the true Benjamin is going to rise up in the Church and declare the magnificence and glory of Jesus, our Lord.

If you can picture that scene in the Bible, in Genesis 43, where Joseph's family had all congregated in Pharaoh's Hall, this has to be one of the most stirring stories of all time. They did not know who Joseph was, but Joseph knew who they were. I believe there is coming a time, very shortly, where churches are going to get together, but because of a lack of spiritual things, I believe that we are going to see a replay of that scene. Scripture says Joseph lifted up his eyes and saw his brother Benjamin, his mother's other son. He asked, "Is this your youngest brother of whom you told me?" Then, he said, "May God be gracious to you." And he made haste to exit the hall, for his bowels did yearn upon his brother. As he sought for a place to weep, he entered into his chambers and there he wept. He was overjoyed with seeing his family together at last. As Joseph knew Benjamin, I see a picture here today of how Jesus knows the members of His Church, but they do not know Him; I believe that this is about to change again. We see a picture, where Joseph revealed himself to his brothers. I believe that we are going to see that again when Christ is going to reveal Himself to His Church. There is going to be a whole lot of repenting going on. Once again, Jesus will show how much He loves us by for-giving us of our transgressions towards Him. There is going to be one more revival before the Lord comes back to take His Church away. I believe it is closer than we think.

There is one more thing the Church needs to experience. When the Lord comes by His Spirit to wake up the Church and bring on a revival, the Spirit of God will manifest the power of God to and through His Church. There is a revelation in Genesis 44:2; you need to read the story to get the full impact of what happened. Joseph told his servants to put his silver cup in the mouth of Benjamin's sack. And then he sent his servants to intercept them. He told them to look for the silver cup and where they would find it. My friends, we could write a book on that statement right there, but I will cut it down for you. This is a type of Christ sending the Holy Spirit to His Church, and He is looking to see who possesses the Spirit. He knows where He sent it, He knows where Pentecost happened, and He knows where to go looking for Pentecost. Those who have experienced Pentecost are going to come under some strict scrutiny. There is going to be a tremendous amount of explaining that will take place. This is a picture of the Church getting its priorities straight, repenting for what they have done, and getting themselves in a position to receive blessing. This ministry will recognize who Jesus is and present Him to the world as He is. The Church is going to experience its own Gethsemane, just as Jesus did: "Take this cup from me but, nevertheless, if this is Your will, Lord, I will drink it."

This Benjamin ministry is a fivefold ministry, a spiritual, governmental ministry. The Church of Jesus Christ should be the most disciplined group of people on this earth. Joseph gave Benjamin five portions of food from his own table and five changes of raiments from his wardrobe. Apostle, prophet, evangelist, pastor, and teacher—these ministering gifts are given to the Church by Jesus Christ Himself, to bring the Church together into a unity of the faith. No longer will the Church be ruled by its five senses. Jesus Christ Himself, being the head of the Church, is going to run the Church that He is building, by inhabiting it Himself. Those churches who do not believe in this five-fold ministry are going to find themselves facing Jesus and explaining to Him why. This is the picture we see back in Genesis.

Yes, see I had nothing to do with being called into this ministry. Jesus put His cup in my sack (this gift and calling) as prophet, so it has been my responsibility to go through the Scriptures, seeking the Lord to explain what "this cup" is all about. Death is not coming without life being reborn; the Word of God will not fall to the ground but will accomplish what it was sent for; the spiritual famine that exists in the Church today is over. I believe there is lots of corn/bread (spiritual food) for the Church. In my studies, I have noticed where some great men and women of God have come to the point of making this declaration and backed off. It makes you weep when you realize how close we are, and yet, how far we are, folks. The Lord is about to reveal Himself to the Church in an awesome way. Yes, we have seen miracles and things that make us wonder. I have told you a few stories from my own experience, but I believe the best is yet to come. Villages and towns and cities are going to see the wind of the Holy Spirit sweep through them, cleansing, healing, and delivering people from their sin, their sicknesses, and diseases. This pandemic that we are experiencing right now will be eliminated by the power of God that is in the Church. We have to step up to these challenges and show the world why we are Christians, and how much God really loves them.

It is time to arise and shine for the light has come and the glory of the Lord has risen upon the Church. Darkness is covering the earth and gross darkness, the people and Benjamin who has that spirit of the wolf hunts at night. (We, as Christians, live in a dark world, and we bring light into the darkness which exposes all the things that are hidden in the dark.) He works when it is dark, He works in the dark, and He will tear apart the works of Satan and cause the sun to shine once again from the Church. There are those that will come and say, "Who do you think you are?" And we will be able to declare, "We are the Church of Jesus Christ, Who came into the world to save sinners and set captives free, to bring peace and joy to a suffering and desperate people." Yes, we are that Church.

Every gate is a pearl and, if you want to be part of this ministry, you are going to go through a lot of irritation; you are going to overcome many things, even death itself; and those who have decided to ignore you, will have to come and bring you with them to see Jesus. Only because Benjamin was with Joseph did he reveal himself to his family, and only because Benjamin was sent by his father to Egypt did the purposes of God get fulfilled. In the fullness of time God sent forth His Son, and in the fullness of time God will send forth Benjamin. The denomination that brings forth this ministry will have to die, just like Rachael did, in order for the ministry to be manifested.

Lessons I have learned:

1. Do not tell your half-brothers your vision.

2. You will only find Jesus when you are with Benjamin.

3. The question remains, are you a half-brother to Jesus or a full brother?

4. You will know them by their fruit.

CHAPTER 11

Thank You, Lord

Let me start off by giving thanks to the Lord for allowing me to experience life from its raw beginnings to this stage, whereby I can share my experiences with the Lord, from my heart, and feel that there has been some meaning beyond myself.

I was born in Nova Scotia in the middle of the Second World War in 1943. I am the eleventh child of a family of twelve. I have seven brothers and four sisters. We are all getting older. Two of my brothers and two of my sisters have gone to be with the Lord. We grew up in a little village called Lower Vaughans. My dad had a lumber business and a woodlot. We grew the majority of our own food. Life was very simple for us at the time. It was not appreciated as much as it is today. Life today is very complicated and very difficult for a lot of people. I have lived where we had nothing, and grew up in a world that seems unlimited in its resources. We were a close family; our neighbours were all part of our family. We went to church every Sunday, and church was very much a part of the village life. My parents, along with some other families in Nova Scotia, were very much a part of the Apostolic vision coming to Canada. There were the Coldwells, the Rands, the Jordans, the Levys, the Cards, the Lytles; these are some of the families that I remember.

They started what is now known as the Apostolic Church in Canada, so I grew up with a Christian background, for which I am very grateful today. At the time I was not so appreciative. I thought that my parents were too restrictive, so I left school, and went away from home with my Grade 8 certificate in hand, to become the champion of the world.

I got a job with the landscaping firm laying sod, picking stones, and shovelling dirt. They paid me money for doing this. At the beginning, it seemed like that was all that mattered. I soon realized that when I became fifty or sixty years of age, I would not be able to do this type of work. So I decided to get some more education. I took correspondence courses to learn what my job was all about. The owner of the company was very gracious. In fact, he saw what I was doing and rewarded me accordingly. He promoted me from stone picking to the position of foreman, superintendent and, finally, general superintendent. We were building golf courses, theme parks, and every line of landscape construction in between. We were very, very, busy. I lived in Markham, Ontario, in an upper-class community. Although we were very busy, we lived a very comfortable life.

In 1979, my youngest daughter was diagnosed with a degenerating eye disease that would take her sight. From the time she was diagnosed until she lost her sight, was only a period of about four months. We were devastated, and we did not know what to do. One morning, I was in my office putting everything in order, planning to go to my boss, and explain to him that I was leaving the company, as I was unable to function and carry out my duties at work because of this terrible disease. I was standing alongside my desk, trying to put together the words of how to tell him this, when I heard an audible voice. All it said was, "Hammond." This was early in the morning around 6:00 a.m. and there was no one else in the building. Something very, very strange had just happened. I had just heard the voice of God. Somehow, inside of me, I knew this was a man of God and I had to find him. To cut a long story short, by 8:30 that morning, I was in this man's office and he was praying with me the Sinner's Prayer. This was how I got saved, and this was the day I committed my life to the Lord. Within three months, twelve members of our family had come to know the Lord as their Saviour. This became the beginning of the rest of my life.

I became very involved in the church, and was totally committed, to the point where I left my secular job. I went into full-time ministry, and within four short years, I was released to go and plant the church in Nova Scotia. I became very committed, totally dedicated, yet completely undisciplined during this time and, as a result, after fourteen years, I burned out. We went back to the construction business that we were familiar with for the next eight years. It was then I felt the Lord calling us to the Assembly here in Gravenhurst, where we are today. The key to everything I experienced in serving the Lord was, to hear the Lord's voice and obey it. I was beginning to understand the meaning of "My sheep know My voice and another they will not follow; they that are born of the Spirit of the Lord should be led by the Spirit of the Lord; and if the same Spirit dwells in you that raised Christ from the dead, He will quicken your mortal body and reveal Himself to you." These are statements Jesus made along with, "Greater is He that is in you than he that is in the world, and greater works will you do than I have done." The second key in this experience was learning what Jesus meant when He said, "I only do the things My Father tells me." "My yoke is easy, My burden is light." These verses have been the guiding principle for me on this journey.

I have so many things to be thankful for, and so many people to be grateful to. I feel compelled to mention a few that have been so instrumental in helping me find my way to where I am. God has been so gracious in demonstrating His love towards us. We can never thank Him enough. People like Stanley Hammond, David Morris, John Carr, David Edwards, Kelly Varner, John Rodham, Jim Watt, Judson Cornwall, George Veitch, and Sunny Salter; Rose Dowling, Gail Crosby, Ruth Johnson, and my Mother—just to mention a few of the many people God has used in my journey, to assist me to grow in grace and to share the good news of the Gospel, which I still believe is the greatest thing we can do.

I thought about this a lot, of giving acknowledgment to those who have helped me along the way. There are many others, and it is hard to mention everybody, but I believe the most important people in my life were my parents. I remember the day I left home. My Mom and Dad hated to see me leave. My Dad called me back to himself for one final word. I will never forget it. He said, "Edwin, live a life so they won't have to lie about you when they bury you." At sixteen years old, I did not quite understand the magnitude of wisdom my father had just given me. But I know that there were many times before I was saved, when temptations would knock at the door of my life and I would hear those words of my father. My father passed away not knowing whether I was saved or not because, at that time I was not serving the Lord. But how I appreciate, over the years, my memories of such a wonderful man.

I realized King Solomon was right when he said that there was nothing new under the sun. Some things can look brand-new after many years. When I think of the things that my mentors have given me, the richness of their time spent with the Lord and given to me is what you will find in this book. For without their dedication and commitment to study and determination to share the Word, I would not be as rich as I am in spiritual matters. Many of the things I have shared are things I have gleaned and learned from these men and women in my life, not forgetting the most important people in my life—my wife Denise (of fifty-six years), my daughters Sherri (her husband, Stephen), and Lisa. Every one of these people, God has used to shape my life and help me to become what I am today. I say thank you and praise God for you.

So, if you read something you may have said when you may have preached, in any way, shape, or form, I apologize for not getting your permission, because I didn't write down at the time who said what. But I have certainly remembered the words that were spoken. If I could remember who spoke, I would give you personal credit, but know that your words have rested in my spirit as nuggets of gold in silver trays. I say join with me as that word continues to grow and go forth to accomplish what it was meant to do for the Kingdom of God. It is not my intention to steal anybody's revelation and claim it as my own. I am just simply sharing the Word of the Lord and what it has done for me, and what it can do when it is used for His glory. There are lives hanging in the balance, waiting to be rescued, and it is my desire to see many souls brought into the Kingdom. I pray that anyone who reads this book, if you do not know the Lord as your personal Saviour and Lord, that you would consider it right now. We all share the truth of the Gospel and the revelation God gives us on our journey, in the hope that we might win some souls from the awfulness of sin, so that they may enjoy the life that Christ died on the cross for, and gave us. He said, *"I have come that you might have life and have it more abundantly"* (John 10:10, NKJV).

There is a huge cloud of witnesses in heaven cheering us on, that we may win this race and join them with millions of others in heaven. God bless you all.